REFLECTIONS

A collection of photographs from the BBC Hulton Picture Library

EDITED BY

NIGEL HARRIS

Silver Link Publishing

5 Hawk Street, Carnforth, Lancashire, LA5 9LA

LNER Reflections: A Collection
of Photographs from the BBC Hulton
Picture Library

1. London and North Eastern Railway
I. Harris, Nigel.
385'.094I   HE3020.L64
ISBN 0 947971 03 3

Copyright Silver Link Publishing & BBC Hulton Picture
Library, 1985. ©

First published in the United Kingdom, September
1985.

ISBN 0 947971 03 3

Designed by Nigel Harris.
Front cover design by Phil Cousins.

Typeset by Dentset, Oxford.
Printed in the United Kingdom by Netherwood Dalton &
Co. Ltd, Huddersfield, Yorkshire.

LNER REFLECTIONS

A collection of photographs from the BBC Hulton Picture Library

Acknowledgements

THE idea for this book originally sprang from a research visit to the BBC Hulton Picture Library whose collection of more than eight million photographs covering many domestic and international topics, contains a very substantial railway section of high quality and great interest. From the railway pictures in the HPL files, 'LNER Reflections' has been painstakingly compiled with the assistance of many individuals and groups, to whom Silver Link Publishing extends its appreciation.

Our thanks first of all to Janet Andrew, Head of BBC Data Services & Sales, BBC Hulton Picture Library Manager David Lee and Acting Manager Bob Bright, and BBC Data Marketing Manager Peter Elliott, who all gave freely of help and advice at every stage from concept to finished product. At the BBC Hulton Picture Library we would like to thank Deputy Manager Roger Wemyss-Brooks and the helpful band of friendly Picture Assistants for invaluable help during the lengthy research period. A very special word of thanks to Senior Picture Assistant Anna Shepherd, who took on much extra work in providing photographs, information and expert guidance around the library's very extensive files.

Whilst the photography in these pages is invariably splendid, some of the original captions provided limited information about the scene portrayed and consequently we turned for more detailed descriptions of the photographs to a panel of LNER experts led by G. J. Hughes, author of two related books and editor of the Gresley Society's journal, 'The Gresley Observer'. Special credit is due to this knowledgeable panel who tackled their job with skill and efficiency, and we would especially like to express our gratitude to Doug Brown, Chris Duffell, David Jackson, Eric Neve, Norman Newsome, Donald Shadbolt, John Watling, Willie Yeadon and of course Geoff Hughes, who co-ordinated the whole exercise.

Other contributors include E. S. Cox and D. R. Carling, whose texts add much to the interest of the book.

Finally, many thanks to Derek Mercer, who did a marvellous job of printing the negatives, and to the Earl of Lichfield for writing the Foreword overleaf.

FRONT COVER: GCR 4-6-0 (LNER class B3) No. 6167 makes an impressive departure from King's Cross with the 'Harrogate Pullman' in 1925. This locomotive was originally named *Lloyd George* but this politician was evidently not in favour with LNER management at the time for when No. 6167 was rostered to take a train conveying Queen Mary to Harrogate, orders were issued for the name plate to be removed before the 4-6-0 entered King's Cross station. This was easier said than done for the brass nameplates were constructed as integral parts of the wheel splasher beading and the work could not be completed in time. It is unlikely that the Queen was aware of these proceedings!

PREVIOUS PAGE: It's August 4 1934 and a busy scene at King's Cross station throat as packed holiday trains prepare to leave London. Left to right are: 'Pacific' No. 2746 *Fairway* (coupled to two 'Atlantics') which has arrived from 'Top Shed'; No. 2598 *Blenheim* with the 'Junior Scotsman' and No. 2795 *Call Boy*, coupled to the 'Flying Scotsman'. An N7 0-6-2T is on the right, in platform 11.

FACING PAGE: The LNER always exploited the maximum publicity value of rostering No. 4472 *Flying Scotsman* to haul the 'Flying Scotsman' train whenever possible and this engine is seen here on July 17 1933, waiting to depart with the first 'non-stop' of the season from platform 10.

BACK COVER: A superb head-on view of No. 2509 *Silver Link* which emphasises the impact this marvellous locomotive must have had when it appeared in 1935. The pioneer 'A4' is seen in pristine ex-works condition, straight from the erecting shop, the tender not yet coaled. The three shades of grey are clearly seen: note that the number was not painted on the buffer beam until the engine had been in service for some time.

FOREWORD

by the Rt. Hon. The Earl of Lichfield, FBIPP, FRPS

IN TODAY'S highly technological world, news images are captured in glowing colour by teams of film and video cameramen and flashed around the world within seconds, via satellite links, giving people on opposite sides of the planet the opportunity to see important events as they occur.

It was not so in the years that the majority of the pictures in this book were taken. Newsreel companies did indeed produce moving pictures of very important events, but generally it was the monochrome photographer, encumbered with heavy, bulky equipment, who carried the responsibility for presenting pictures of the news to the British public. These were the classic years of the photographic agency, such as the Topical Press Agency, which produced many of the fine pictures reproduced to such high standards in this collection of images from the BBC Hulton Picture Library.

The Agency photographers were always on hand to record the latest developments and innovations from the private railway companies who were acutely aware of the need to present themselves in the best possible light. With intense competition for business in passenger and goods markets, companies like the LNER regularly hosted gatherings of press photographers and their work presents some fascinating reflections of the LNER, particularly in the 1930s, frequently regarded as the 'Golden Age' of Britain's railways. The railway enthusiast will find much of interest in these pages: the photographs cover everything from crack expresses and their locomotives to uniforms, signals, carriages and accidents. Every picture fascinates, for even when you've absorbed all aspects of the main subject, the wealth of detail visible in the picture backgrounds will continue to hold your attention. From the viewpoint of railway history this book offers important insights — some of them quite new — into the ways and operations of the LNER. Furthermore, in an age when some period photographs are becoming rather well-known, this collection contains many images which are published here for the first time.

In the wider view however this book will appeal far beyond the interests of the railway enthusiast alone. In the period illustrated here the railway was the mass public carrier: everyone and almost all goods went just about everywhere by train. The private car was only for the well-to-do, commercial air travel was in its infancy and the railway was held in public esteem in much the same way that air and space travel is today. The railway's locomotives and equipment represented the very peak of technical and scientific achievement and the express drivers were the social elite, heroes of similar status to the *Concorde* or space-shuttle pilots of the modern age. In these bygone years, major family and domestic events for British people nearly always involved emotional scenes under railway station clocks from King's Cross to Crianlarich: the railway was inextricably woven into the very fabric of British life. As such this collection of photographs opens a fascinating window onto another vanished aspect of British life. Railwaymen were intensely proud and loyal to their companies, whose magnificent locomotives — especially the graceful 'streamliners' — epitomised everything that was Great about Britain, the country which gave the iron road to the world. Trains, and particularly the steam locomotive, will always command a special place in the affections of the British people and these pictures provide an evocative recollection of a treasured period. It is equally importantly a worthy tribute to the skills of a hardy breed of photographers who enjoyed the benefits of little of the sophistication of equipment available to us today, but who produced work of very good quality. Their photographs are to be savoured!

'Silver Link'
and the
'Silver Jubilee'

IN 1933 the German railways introduced a two-car streamlined diesel train, running between Berlin and Hamburg — known as 'The Flying Hamburger' — and this had drawn international attention to the possibilities of rail services running at considerably higher average speeds than were usual at the time. The LNER gave consideration to a similar service to operate between King's Cross, London and Newcastle upon Tyne, but decided that a suitably modified steam-hauled train could provide a better solution than diesel traction. The result was the streamlined 'Silver Jubilee' train, introduced by the LNER on September 30 1935, for which Chief Mechanical Engineer H. N. Gresley (who was knighted the following year, becoming Sir Nigel Gresley) built four specially designed 'Pacific' locomotives. Although basically similar in concept to his earlier 'Pacifics' the new class had a number of significant modifications, aimed principally at improving steaming, but the most striking change was the overall appearance of the new engines. The entire locomotive was enclosed in a silver-grey streamlined casing, a mode which was continued in the external finish of the 'Silver Jubilee' coaches, giving the train an impressive, uniform appearance. The new locomotives were built at the LNER's Doncaster works, four being constructed to haul the 'Silver Jubilee' train in the closing months of 1935. The first to emerge was No. 2509 *Silver Link*, seen (above left) at an advanced stage of construction. The final touches are being put to the streamlined casing — note the fitter trimming a hole with a circular file, while his companion on the floor prepares mountings for the valances covering the coupled wheels. Note also that cast nameplates had been made and fitted to the 'Pacific' at this stage, though it was later decided that the engine's appearance would be enhanced by the name being painted on the boiler sides and this was carried out before *Silver Link* entered service. Manufacture of the cladding plates for the A4 class was a task requiring great skill: note the complex curvature of the final piece needed above the buffer — and each piece had to be specially made as no patterns were available. The official works view (left) of *Silver Link* captures superbly the striking appearance of the new 'Pacific', which was still carrying its nameplates. *Silver Link* was painted silver-grey, with battleship grey for the side valances and charcoal grey on the front of the smokebox. There was no lining out and the letters and numbers were silver, shaded in blue, in contrast to the usual red-shaded gold lettering of the green liveried locomotives.

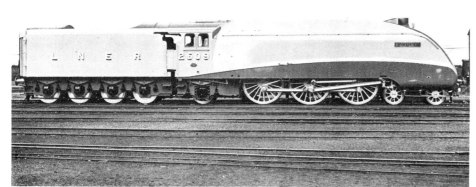

Right: A detail view of *Silver Link* shortly before entry into traffic and after removal of the nameplate in favour of the painted name on the boiler cladding plates: the mounting holes for the nameplates have been carefully filled. Towards the end of 1937 the LNER decided to paint all the streamlined 'Pacifics' in garter blue livery, and when *Silver Link* was repainted in December of that year the nameplates were restored. Unlike the remainder of the class, the nameplates of the first two engines *Silver Link* and *Quicksilver*, had rounded, rather than square corners. As compared with the photograph on page 5, this view clearly shows an early modification to the livery: the charcoal grey of the smokebox front has been carried round onto the sides in a graceful curve, thus emphasizing the streamlined engine's sleek character. The small sliding panels in the valances over the wheels gave drivers access to the motion for lubrication purposes. The small hole in the cylinder casing above the leading bogie wheel was for the hand-operated crank used to open and close the 'cod's mouth' panel on the front of the locomotive, to give access to the conventional smokebox door hidden behind the streamlined nose.

Above left: The chime whistle is fitted to *Silver Link* in the Doncaster works erecting shop, as the locomotive approaches completion in the summer of 1935. The recessed drawgear fitted to the first four A4 'Pacifics' was not perpetuated on later-built locomotives as it resulted in insufficient space for a man to stand in safety to couple up when the locomotive was buffered up to its train. In the background is the second A4 of the batch, No. 2510 *Quicksilver*, awaiting the fitting of boiler cladding plates over the heat insulation lagging.

Above right: At an earlier stage of construction, a boiler-maker is caulking a seam inside the copper firebox, which was extended forwards to form a combustion chamber: this feature increased the size of the firebox heating surface; as a result the length of the boiler tubes was reduced. The small holes in the tubeplate will accomodate 121 boiler tubes, while the 43 larger holes will carry the flue tubes and superheater elements. With the exception of Gresley's 'Hush-Hush' No. 10000, the 'A4s' introduced 250psi boiler pressure to the LNER for the first time. The earlier A3 'Pacifics' worked at 220psi. The streamlined 'Pacific's' firebox had a heating surface of 231 sq.ft. within a total heating surface (including flues and tubes) of 3,325 sq.ft. The firegrate area was 41.25 sq.ft.

Above: On a rather grey day at King's Cross, No. 2509 *Silver Link* makes an impressive, if smoky start with the trial 'Silver Jubilee' of September 27 1935. The innovative locomotive and train clearly made a striking impression amidst the more familiar engines and stock. During this trial run to Barkston, near Grantham, to which the press were invited, *Silver Link* achieved a British speed record when it accelerated the train to 112½ mph. this speed being verified by several observers — including Gresley himself. *Silver Link* established further records for steam and diesel traction by running at an average of 107.5mph for 25 miles; an average of 100.6mph for 41 miles 15 chains and 100mph or over continuously for approximately 43 miles. Driver Taylor and Fireman Luty were in charge of *Silver Link*, which gained 10 minutes on its timing to Peterborough — just over one quarter of the distance to Newcastle — thus illustrating the locomotive's reserve of speed in normal running. The 'Silver Jubilee' was booked to run the 232¼ miles from King's Cross to Newcastle in just four hours in each direction at an average speed of nearly 70mph, with maximum speeds of 90mph required for considerable distances.

Above left: A gathering of dignitaries are photographed alongside No. 2509 *Silver Link* at King's Cross, after the 'Pacific' had arrived with the inaugural public trip of the 'Silver Jubilee' at 2pm on September 30 1935. Lord Mayor of London Sir Stephen Killick is seen with the Sheriffs of the City of London, the Lord Mayor of Newcastle upon Tyne and the Mayor of Darlington. Today's IC 125s echo the shape of the A4s at King's Cross, thus perpetuating and improving the image of high speed travel established by the LNER 50 years ago.

Above right: The 6ft 5in diameter tapered boiler barrel has been fitted to the firebox in the Doncaster works boiler shop and compressed air rivetting and caulking hammers are being used to complete the boiler eventually used on streamlined 'Pacific' No. 2511 *Silver King* — the third locomotive of the original batch of four. The boiler barrel carries the painted identification 'Bo. 821 A4 No. 3.'

Right: No. 2509 *Silver Link* rests at King's Cross shed — or 'Top Shed' as it was better known — during a fortnight of trials carried out before it commenced regular scheduled work on 'The Silver Jubilee', which was operated by the LNER to commemorate the jubilee of the reign of King George V. The train was booked to leave Newcastle at 10 am, stopping only at Darlington before running to King's Cross, where it was due to arrive at 2 pm. The return journey was timed to leave London at 5.30 pm, reaching Darlington at 8.45 pm and Newcastle at 9.30 pm. All seats were reservable, supplementary fares being charged at 5/− (25p) first class and 3/− (15p) second class, and the train was generally filled to capacity.

Below: An unidentified A4 'Pacific' under construction at Doncaster works, also on April 26 1938. The sloping smokebox top and the unusual shape of the smokebox door — not normally visible — are clearly apparent in this view. Note that the running plate is not entirely curved on the 'aerofoil' section just ahead of the cylinders, where there is a distinctly flatter section. The linkage forming part of Gresley's conjugated mechanism for operating the valves of the inside cylinder can be seen ahead of the valve chest above the outside cylinder.

Above: It's April 26 1938 at Doncaster works and a welder is busy completing the beading arund the cab windows of No. 4500 *Garganey* (named after a wildfowl of the duck family), works No. 1873. Several of the later 'A4's' were named after wild birds, but in some cases these were later replaced by the names of LNER personages. *Garganey* was renamed *Sir Ronald Matthews*, who succeeded William Whitelaw as LNER Chairman in 1938. When LNER locomotives were renumbered in 1946 the A4 'Pacifics' began the numerical list and No. 4500 became No. 1, and following Nationalisation No. 60001. It was stationed at Gateshead all its life and was not often seen in London. Another part-built 'A4' is visible on the left.

No 4499
CLASS A·4

Top: A further 31 streamlined 'Pacifics' were completed at Doncaster between December 1936 and July 1938: this was one of the last to be built. 'Alfol' heat insulation is being applied to the boiler; blocks of the material are being strapped around the barrel while mattresses are being fitted to the firebox. The centre driving wheel splasher is normally hidden behind the streamlining. The new 'A4' in the background is at a slightly more advanced stage.

Above and left: Because of heavy traffic expected for the Scottish Empire Exhibition, held at Glasgow in 1938, LNER passenger services were strengthened and the non-stop 'Flying Scotsman' was booked to run on Sundays, as well as weekdays from July 4. Two new teak-panelled trains were built at the Carriage Works at Doncaster for the non-stop services, featuring pressure ventilation and including provision for buffet meals in addition to the full restaurant car service. Also destined for this service was the last batch of the streamlined 'Pacifics' built in the first half of 1938, including No. 4499 Pochard. This locomotive was also named after a variety of wild bird and was renamed the following year after LNER Deputy Chairman Sir Murrough Wilson, a director of the LNER and NER since 1912. The recessed drawhook had been abandoned by this stage.

Above: King's Cross station was completed in 1852 to the design of Lewis Cubitt, who planned the station along the lines of a riding school which had been recently built in Moscow for the Russian Tzar. The station, which opened on October 14 1852, cost around £123,000 to construct and originally featured two long platforms separated by 16 tracks, 14 of which were used for stabling rolling stock. The double-arched building was 800 feet in length, 210 feet wide and 71 feet high, and at the time of construction the station roof was probably the biggest of its kind in the world. The facade of yellow London bricks was crowned by a clock tower which contained three bells, the heaviest of which weighed 1½ tons. The clock had four faces originally, but one could not be seen as it faced out over the train sheds and its figures were eventually painted out and its mechanism removed. Sufficient for the requirements of its time, King's Cross became increasingly inadequate for the growing needs of travellers. Additional platforms were added at the western side but the lack of circulating space meant that passenger congestion at busy times would never be avoided, whilst many difficulties were placed in the way of the operating staff by conflicting traffic movements and the complex trackwork at the station approach. The exterior of the station, attractive in its simplicity, was spoiled in LNER days by the unsightly clutter of shops and office buildings constructed in front of the facade, including, in this 1929 view, the Piccadilly 'tube' building, which utilised rhubarb coloured bricks. This complex became known as 'the African village'.

Above: A view of the King's Cross station throat, looking back towards the platforms from Gas Works tunnel. The complexity of the trackwork at the station exit is clearly shown; no fewer than five double slips and one single slip are visible, together with one four-way point behind the catwalk support on the right. Space was very cramped and trains entering the suburban platforms, just off the right of the picture, blocked all access to the main platforms. To minimise movements between the station and 'Top Shed', the entrance to which was between Gas Works and Copenhagen tunnels, locomotives were frequently coupled together in twos and threes whilst moving to and from the shed. In LNER days the suburban tank engines invariably worked with smokeboxes facing north: here is an N2 0-6-2T in company with an Ivatt 'Atlantic' on June 1 1934.

Left: Platform 1 at King's Cross on May 7 — the fourth day of the General Strike — and the station is becoming congested with empty milk churns, awaiting return to the dairies. The glass-lined milk tank wagons introduced in 1928 eventually displaced the churn although it was many years before the clatter of a milk churn, expertly wheeled by a porter, vanished completely from the railway scene. Worthy of note in this cameo of 60 years ago are the enamelled iron signs advertising Stephens Ink and Bravington's Rings as well as the gas lanterns, converted to electricity by this time. This was the arrival side of the station — platforms 1, 2, and 5 being full length, Nos. 3 and 4 being shorter, No. 3 being let into No. 4. Later the island platform was widened and platform 3 disappeared, No. 4 thus becoming full length.

Below: It's May 11 1926 during the General Strike and every platform at King's Cross from No. 11 to No. 14 is occupied. On the left is class K2 No. 4640, the first of Gresley's large boiler two-cylinder 2-6-0s, built at Doncaster in 1914. Locomotives in this class were modified with cut-down boiler mountings to work over the GE and NB sections, but No. 4640 still has its tall chimney and Ramsbottom safety valves. The three condenser-fitted class N2 0-6-2Ts (left to right) Nos. 4732, 4745 and 4737 are all from the batch of 50 built by the North British Locomotive Co. in 1920/21. In the previous year the LNER had spent £10,000 on improving passenger facilities at King's Cross, including the provision of underground bathrooms, lavatories, hair dressing salons and a new Enquiry Office.

These two photographs, taken with only a brief interval between them in August 1925, show the preparations (above) for the departure of the 11.20am Harrogate and Edinburgh Pullman train from platform 10 at King's Cross. The empty coaches have been brought into the station by an N2 0-6-2T, whilst on platform 6 (below) passengers are waiting for the coaches of another down express to arrive. At this time King's Cross did not have a full length platform between Nos. 6 and 10, only non-platform tracks for the short-term storage of stock, though No. 8 had a short platform for the loading of road vehicles into vans with end doors. In this road can be seen a clerestory roofed bogie coach, a van and two horseboxes; alongside this short platform are parked a pair of low-roofed non-corridor GNR coaches. On the opposite side of the platform (No. 7) a twin-cylinder gas wagon rests against the buffer stops. Note the scissors crossover and the raised walkway between the tracks, provided to help cleaning staff climb into the carriages. Passenger circulating space at King's Cross was very limited, the end wall of the terminus being only a few yards from the buffer stops. These buffer stops — hydraulically operated and supplied by a special 20,000 gallon cistern on the station roof — were tested every Wednesday between 11am and noon, when a locomotive compressed them one by one until the buffers were pushed home, a gauge registering the pressure required. In 1926 the LNER constructed an additional full length platform between existing platforms 6 and 10 at a cost of £9,000. The platform, which had

two faces to serve two trains simultaneously, was 945ft long and was brought into use on Sunday September 19 1926.

Above: The LNER introduced a Pullman service from King's Cross to Harrogate and Newcastle in 1923. This was successful and in the following year a further Pullman service was started, serving Sheffield and running non-stop as far as Nottingham. Here we see Ivatt 'Atlantic' No. 4426 drawing away from platform 10 with the inaugural 'Sheffield Pullman' at 11.05am on June 2 1924. The train was not well patronised and in an effort to attract more passengers the journey times were reversed after a few weeks, the train running up from Sheffield at 10.30am and returning from King's Cross at 6.05pm. However, this proved to be no more successful and when the Pullman services were revised in September 1925 Sheffield and Nottingham were dropped from the schedules. Note the GNR type ground signals.

Left, above: The inaugural Sheffield Pullman of June 2 1924 disappears into Gas Works tunnel. The train comprised: one first class car seating 22 passengers, and four third class cars with capacity for a further 130 people.

Left, below: Soon after the Grouping of 1923, W. G. P Maclure was appointed Locomotive Running Superintendent of the Southern Area of the LNER, comprising the Great Central, Great Eastern and Great Northern sections. Maclure had occupied a similar position on the GCR and at his instigation a number of the largest class B3 GCR 4-6-0s were transferred to King's Cross shed to assist in working the Pullman services. The first of the B3s was named *Lord Faringdon* after the chairman of the GCR Board, and who later became the first Deputy Chairman of the LNER. The locomotive was built at the GCR works at Gorton, Manchester, in 1917 and was followed in 1920 by five others. They were numbered 6164 to 6169 and here we see No.6166 *Earl Haig* at King's Cross in charge of a Pullman train for Harrogate, on May 3 1926.

THE LNER made the most of publicising its non-stop 'Flying Scotsman' service, which started running between King's Cross and Edinburgh on May 1 1928, although it is interesting to note that earlier in the year the company had refused to confirm that the new non-stop run would commence in 1928. In a style still common today, the LNER had said that the summer services were 'yet to be considered' and that no drastic changes would be made before April — the Board clearly did not want to dilute the impact of the publicity to be had when the service actually started. Modifications to the valve arrangements of selected 'Pacifics' gave more economical running, enabling them to cover the 392½ miles to Waverley without running out of coal. Also, the redesigned tender, incorporating a side corridor, enabled the crew to be changed en route, without stopping. Nevertheless the original schedule still brought the non-stop into Waverley at 6.15pm — an average speed of only 47½mph. This was because of a long standing agreement with the West Coast partnership dating back to the Race to Aberdeen 30 years previously. The departure of the first non-stop, on May 1 1928 was an occasion for great crowds at King's Cross and No. 4472 *Flying Scotsman* itself was rostered to inaugurate the first down service from London. Here we see two views of the train just as it is starting away from platform 10, together with a third view of the train about to enter Gas Works tunnel. The leading coaches form the through portion to Aberdeen, those in the picture being brake third No. 1055 and a third class compartment coach, both built at York in 1924, especially for the 'Flying Scotsman' service.

Left: The non-stop 'Flying Scotsman' was worked on alternate days by 'Pacifics' stationed at King's Cross and Haymarket respectively. On July 8 1929 No. 2566 *Ladas* (the Scottish engine concerned) worked the first non-stop of the season up to London, returning on the down working the following day. *Ladas* had exchanged its original Great Northern tender for one of the corridor tenders only a few days before commencing its non-stop diagram, and is seen leaving King's Cross on July 9 1929, next stop Edinburgh Waverely. In 1929 about 60,000 passengers passed through King's Cross each day.

Below: Five minutes after *Ladas* had departed with the non-stop 'Flying Scotsman', No. 2578 *Bayardo* starts the relief train, popularly known as the 'Junior Scotsman' from platform 8. Bayardo was shedded at Heaton and would work the train to Newcastle. Three other 'Pacifics' are preparing to leave with No. 4476 *Royal Lancer* on the right, whilst at platform 6 (on the left) is No. 2544 *Lemberg*. This locomotive, together with No. 2578 were amongst the first Gresley 'Pacifics' to be fitted with 220 psi boilers, after which they were reclassified as 'A3s' though at the time the two types were commonly referred to either as 'ordinary' or 'super Pacifics'. The central island platform (platforms 7 and 8) was the narrow, full length platform built by the LNER in 1926 to replace the small end-loading platform adjacent to the buffer stops, and increase passenger capacity.

Right: King's Cross by night. With steam roaring from the safety valves, No. 4474 *Victor Wild* strains at the leash with the down 'Aberdonian', with through sleeping coaches for Aberdeen, on March 23 1931. The somersault signal adjacent to the back of the tender indicates that the road is clear — but instead of watching for the guard's signal, Driver Bartaby and the well-wishers at the platform end are more interested in the camera! Unlike most of Gresley's non-streamlined 'Pacifics', which were named after winners of classic races, *Victor Wild* commemorated the winner of the Jubilee Handicap of Kempton Park in 1896.

Left: No. 4472 *Flying Scotsman* eases away from platform 10 at King's Cross with the first down non-stop of the 1931 season, on July 20. Just visible on the left of the picture is No. 2573 *Harvester*, from the 1924 batch built by the North British Locomotive Company, and stationed at Gateshead at this time. *Harvester* — named after the joint winner of the 1884 Derby ended in a dead heat — is in charge of the 10.05am departure, also bound for Scotland, but scheduled to stop en route.

Below left: With the somersault arm showing a clear road ahead through Gas Works tunnel on July 20 1931, No. 2573 *Harvester* barks away from platform 8 at King's Cross with the 10.05am 'Junior Scotsman'. The leading coach will run through to Perth. Gas Works 'tunnel' actually consisted of three double-track bores and *Harvester* will veer to the left, taking the right-hand track of the westernmost portal. The LNER was justifiably proud of the 'Pacifics' performance on the non-stop runs, and in 1931 the Company announced that on Saturday August 16 No. 2795 *Call Boy* of Haymarket Shed completed a 28-day diagram of duties between King's Cross and Edinburgh in which time it hauled the 'Flying Scotsman' non-stop on 24 weekdays, in addition to working a stopping express on the four Sundays. In total the engine had covered 11,000 trouble-free miles, including 9,400 miles of 'Flying Scotsman' duties.

Facing page: In May 1932 the tedious 8¼-hour schedule to Edinburgh with the 'Flying Scotsman' was at last accelerated when on May 2 the time to Waverley was cut to 7hr 50min. No. 2750 *Papyrus* — named after the 1923 Derby winner — blasts the underside of the signal gantry as it leaves platform 10 at King's Cross with the first working of the faster schedule, once again admired by a large crowd at the platform end. Non-stop running recommenced in July. Three years later this locomotive reached 108mph whilst hauling a special train from Newcastle to King's Cross.

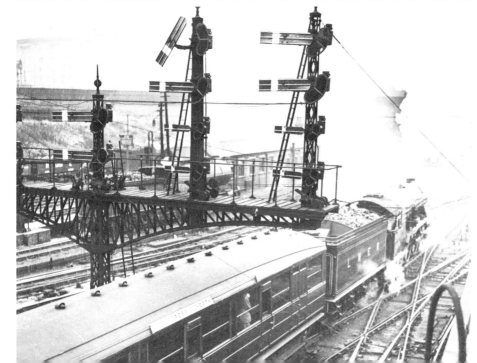

Above: This photograph is something of a mystery. Ivatt 'Atlantic' No. 3278 is purportedly leaving King's Cross on May 2 1932 with a 'Flying Scotsman' working; however, the only reason a main line train would leave from platform 15, in the suburban station, would be for a trial run of some description. At this time No. 3278 had been out of workshops for only a month, and would thus have been in good shape for a high speed run. Platform 15 would only accommodate about half a dozen standard corridor coaches, so the train, apparently of newly refurbished stock, would have been quite short.

Below: The resumption of non-stop running to Edinburgh in July 1932 saw the schedule cut once again, this time to 7½ hours, and No. 4472 *Flying Scotsman* was again rostered to head the inaugural train. Sister 'Pacific' No. 2561 *Minoru* stands alongside with the 'Junior Scotsman'. The overhead catwalk was built prior to the installation of colour light signals, completed in October 1932. The catwalks allowed engineers access to the signals without walking over the tracks of the busy terminus, but they also carried the colour lights themselves and many of their power cables. King's Cross was — and still is — prone to flooding and the LNER was keen to keep as many cables as possible above the 'flooding level'. The prospect of the station being put out of action by waterlogged electrics was unthinkable. The new signalling sytem was controlled by a single electrically operated signal box of 232 levers, which replaced two older manual signal boxes with a total of 240 levers. A pair of N2 and N1 tank engines are just visible in the suburban platforms — note the differing roof profiles.

Left: Bank Holiday periods meant that King's Cross was even busier than usual — especially around 10am as the 'Flying Scotsman' got away. This was the scene during the Easter weekend in 1933, on April 12, as No. 2547 *Donovan* gets to grips with the 9.50am relief to the 'Flying Scotsman' whilst No. 4475 *Flying Fox* awaits the rightaway with the '10am' itself. This will be followed into Gas Works tunnel by No. 2549 *Persimmon*, which is waiting (on the left) at platform 7 with the 10.10am to Leeds. A fourth unidentified 'Pacific' is standing in platform 11 with the 10.20am stopping train known as 'the Parly'. This engine alone stands as pilot for the 'Flying Scotsman' — if the rostered engine should fail for any reason a relief is thus standing ready at the next platform. At platform 12 an N2 0-6-2T heads the 9.50am 'local' to New Barnet: this train will take the slow line through Gas Works tunnel, keeping out of the way of the expresses.

An impressive scene at King's Cross shortly before 10am on August 4 1934. On the left three locomotives coupled together to reduce line occupancy are backing into platform 5: these are 'Pacific' No. 2746 *Fairway* (named after the 1928 St Leger winner) and a pair of 'Atlantics' which have moved from the top shed to the terminus in readiness for their journeys north. No. 2795 *Call Boy* (winner of the 1927 Derby) of Haymarket shed stands ready with the non-stop 'Flying Scotsman' while sister 'Pacific' No. 2598 *Blenheim* (the 1930 Derby winner) of Gateshead shed is at the head of the 'Junior Scotsman'. An N7 0-6-2T of GER design is waiting to leave from platform 11; a number of this class of small-wheeled suburban tanks were stationed at King's Cross for several years for working the branch lines from Hatfield, St Albans, Luton and Hertford. Suburban tank engines were known to King's Cross crews as 'Met' tanks, from their ability to run on the widened lines of the Metropolitan system between King's Cross and Moorgate. The GER N7 types were known as 'Swedy Mets'. Note the fogman's hut in the foreground and the superb four-way point alongside.

Flanked by sister 'Pacific' No. 2750 *Papyrus* and N2 0-6-2T No. 2664, 'A3' No. 2796 *Spearmint* starts the first non-stop Flying Scotsman of the 1934 season from platform 10 at King's Cross on July 9 1934. *Spearmint*, a well-known Haymarket engine which spent its entire working life based in Scotland, was built in 1930 at Doncaster and named after the Derby winner of 1906. The N2 is in charge of the parallel departure of a suburban articulated set — it will probably beat the 'A3' up Holloway bank — while *Papyrus* is coupled to the 'Junior Scotsman'.

'Top Shed'

Above: An interesting and varied line-up of locomotives at 'Top Shed' at King's Cross, nicely posed for the photographer. From left to right: K2 2-6-0 No. 4667, then an unidentified engine inside the gloomy shed, C1 4-4-2 No. 4461 (the last to be built), B3 4-6-0 No. 6167, 'Pacific' No. 2546 *Donovan* and C1 4-4-2 No. 4442. This last engine was used by the GNR to work Royal trains and it had the Great Northern coat of arms painted on its rear splashers.

Above left: The roundhouse at King's Cross shed was the home of the tank engines used for suburban work, and for carriage and goods shunting. In this 1926 scene we see (left to right): Ivatt class J52 0-6-0ST No. 4255, built at Doncaster in 1901, and five 0-6-2Ts. The first two are examples of the batch of 10 class 'N2s' built at Doncaster in 1920/1, whilst the third 0-6-2T is an N2 built by the North British Locomotive Company in the same period. Next comes an N1 0-6-2T and a clear distinction is evident between the classes: the 'N1s' had slide valves whilst the 'N2s' (a later design) had piston valves, the end-covers of which can be seen protruding beneath the smokebox door. This caused the boiler to be carried higher in the frames, resulting in a much more squat chimney, giving the class a more modern appearance. King's Cross roundhouse was demolished in 1931 and replaced by straight roads.

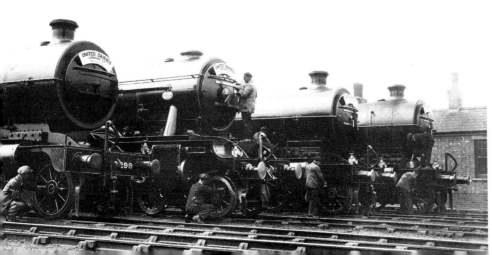

Left: More than 1,000 milk salesmen from United Dairies finished work on June 29 1932 after delivering the usual morning supplies to 200,000 customers, and gathered at King's Cross to join four special trains for a day's outing to Yarmouth. Luncheon and dinner were provided on the trains, the trip being paid for by the milkmen contributing a shilling a week (5p) for three months. The four locomotives shown being prepared at 'Top Shed' for the outing are 'Pacific' No. 4472 *Flying Scotsman* and 'Atlantics' Nos. 3299, 4444 and 3274. However, it is unlikely that 4472 actually hauled one of the trains and this picture was probably set up at the shed merely for publicity purposes. Another photograph shows No. 2546 *Donovan* at King's Cross station, with the headboard attached and surrounded by a crowd of happy milkmen!

Right: During the week-long General Strike of May 1926, skeleton train serices were operated by non-striking railwaymen assisted by volunteer workers from outside the industry. In this scene on May 11 a volunteer fireman (left) is oiling the motion of a class K2 2-6-0. Will he replace that missing bolt securing the running plate to the motion bracket before he sets off? Incidentally, the original caption for this picture states that the volunteer had actually walked from Manchester to London to help the railways during the crisis! The K2 was one of Gresley's earliest designs, and until the larger 'K3s' were built in quantity, they provided the motive power for GN fast freights, as well as secondary passenger and excursion workings. As more 'K3s' were built for these duties, several 'K2s' were drafted to the GE and West Highland lines, where they were a mainstay for many years: indeed they spent longer in Western Scotland than they did on GN metals.

Left: The press photographers and news editors of the mid-1920s were clearly able to work tongue-in-cheek, crisis or not. The original caption for this picture describes these three volunteers as studying their map of the route before setting out with their train! Judging by his cap badge, the man in the centre holding the 'map' has maritime connections. It is unlikely that the trio were studying a route map of the GN main line, but the picture is nevertheless of interest: note the detail of the big-end, small-end and slide bars. The locomotive is 'Atlantic' No. 4455 (works No. 1279) one of the last batch of 10 of these engines built at Doncaster in 1910.

Right: More volunteers at work during the General Strike; the gentleman second from the left, smartly attired in vee-neck pullover, striped shirt and tie looks as though he has left his City office to help the LNER! The men are turning 'Atlantic' No. 4456 on the King's Cross station yard turntable on May 11 1926, during the Strike. Note that even the tender-back is lined and that the red buffer beam has a white edge.

When the 'Pacifics' were first used to King's Cross they were sent out to Ferme Park, Hornsey to turn, as the turntable at 'Top Shed' was too small. In January 1924 new facilities were installed at King's Cross station yard, including a 70ft turntable, and the 4-6-2s were turned there for many years until a large turntable was provided at the shed in 1932.

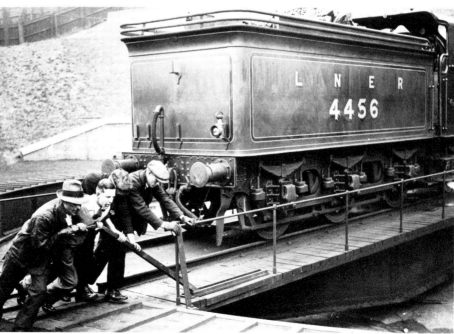

Above: The power of the press! Usually a team of four cleaners under a chargeman was responsible for cleaning a locomotive — here no less than 12 men have been assembled doubtless for the benefit of the photographers, to groom 'Pacific' No. 2597 *Gainsborough* for the down 'Flying Scotsman' of April 10 1933. *Gainsborough* was named after the triple winner of the Derby, 2,000 Guineas and St Leger in 1918, and was built at Doncaster in 1930. At this time of year the 'Flying Scotsman' did not run non-stop and the engine hauling the down train worked as far as Newcastle. *Gainsborough*, based at Gateshead at this time, spent practically all its life allocated in the North Eastern Area.

Left : It would not have been possible for one set of men to work the 'Flying Scotsman' non-stop to Edinburgh from King's Cross, and to have had two crews on the footplate would have meant unneccessary overcrowding. The answer to this problem was found in the corridor tender, through which a relief crew could walk from the train. Here No. 4472 *Flying Scotsman* — one of the first locomotives to receive a corridor tender — poses for the 'Topical' photographer on the turntable at King's Cross. Relief crews heading for the footplate would turn sharp right once inside the tender, and then immediately left to walk down the narrow corridor along the right-hand side. Note the circular 'porthole' to let light into this corridor. The 'A3s' corridor tenders were later transferred to the 'A4s'. The LNER realised that the new tenders would be exchanged between engines and adopted the practice of painting locomotive numbers on the cab sides, instead of the tender sides, as had been the practice since the Grouping.

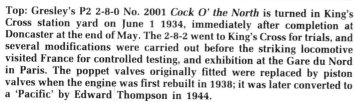

Top: Gresley's P2 2-8-0 No. 2001 *Cock O' the North* is turned in King's Cross station yard on June 1 1934, immediately after completion at Doncaster at the end of May. The 2-8-2 went to King's Cross for trials, and several modifications were carried out before the striking locomotive visited France for controlled testing, and exhibition at the Gare du Nord in Paris. The poppet valves originally fitted were replaced by piston valves when the engine was first rebuilt in 1938; it was later converted to a 'Pacific' by Edward Thompson in 1944.

Above & right: An experimental Cowans & Sheldon appliance was installed at 'Top Shed' in 1934 to enable locomotives to be turned by a vacuum tractor powered by the locomotive's brake ejector. On November 7 1934 'Pacific' No. 2501 *Colombo* is being turned by its fireman.

The GN Section

Ivatt 'Atlantic' No. 1410 takes the down through line at Wood Green with a semi-fast train in July 1923. In the following month this locomotive entered Doncaster works for overhaul, during which it was repainted in LNER livery and numbered 4410. The two leading coaches are early GNR bogie stock. The tall chimney of Barratt's sweet factory can be seen between the engine smokebox and the tall somersault signal, which is fitted with the low level repeater arms.

Right: The second 'P2' 2-8-2 No. 2002 *Earl Marischal* was completed at Doncaster in October 1934 and for some months worked between King's Cross and Doncaster before moving to Scotland in June 1935. No. 2002 is seen here on November 9 1934 approaching Hadley Wood station with an up express. Unlike *Cock O' the North*, No. 2002 was fitted with piston valves from the start, but was otherwise outwardly similar to the class pioneer, except that the steam pipe covers were visible and the ACFI feedwater heater was not fitted. After a few months in service further smoke deflecting plates were fitted outside the original sheeting: the locomotive was later modified with a streamlined casing similar to that of the 'A4s' and it was eventually rebuilt as a non-streamlined 4-6-2 in 1944 by Edward Thompson.

Below: The city of Kingston-upon-Hull enjoyed Pullman services from October 1935 when through coaches for Hull were added to the 'West Riding Pullman' train. The service was accelerated to a 60mph schedule between King's Cross and Doncaster in each direction and the train was renamed the 'Yorkshire Pullman'. No. 2559 *The Tetrach*, of Doncaster shed, is seen entering Hadley Wood tunnel with the up 'Yorkshire Pullman' on October 23 1935.

Left: This page illustrates how the camera can be made to obscure the truth! This picture is quite genuine and depicts a special trip of the 1924 'Flying Scotsman' train, operated for the benefit of the press on September 29 that year. The LNER was always a shrewd operator in the public relations field. New coaches had been built at Doncaster for this train, including facilities for hairdressing, and as the press handout explained, the exclusive use of electricity throughout the train for cooking and lighting, instead of gas. The locomotive is the second of the first pair of 'Pacifics' built to H. N. Gresley's design at Doncaster in 1922, and still with GNR numbering as No. 1471N *Sir Frederick Banbury*. The 'N' suffix designated the engine's origin on the GNR and was used for a time until renumbering took place. Sir Frederick Banbury was the last chairman of the Great Northern Railway, and an implacable opponent of the Grouping.

In 1930 it was announced that the new airship R100 would carry out a programme of overseas flights to Canada and Egypt, and to contrast the two modes of transport, the Topical Press Agency produced in March 1930 a composite photograph. This purported to show R100 overflying the 'Flying Scotsman' as it approached Hatfield. Not only was the airship superimposed onto the 1924 picture, but in admirable attention to detail, the locomotive was also brought up to date! The artist's skills were used to change the numbers on the cabside and bufferbeam to 4471, and to substitute a more modern tender in place of the original GNR type, with coal rails — which No. 4471 in fact retained all its life. However, by 1930 No. 4471's cab and boiler fittings had been reduced in height to conform with the standard LNER loading gauge: perhaps this was beyond the artist's ability!

Facing page, top: An earlier example of class C1 'Atlantic', No. 3286, enters Grantham from the south with a down stopping train of pre-Gresley stock. The first of this class, No. 3251 was completed in December 1902, to be followed by a production batch of 20 further locomotives, Nos. 3272-3291, in 1904. Most of the class were withdrawn before the end of the LNER period, No. 3286 succumbing in October 1947. Class pioneer No. 251 survives in the National Collection at the National Railway Museum, York.

Left: Until enough 'Pacifics' were available to work all the heaviest long-distance trains, the combination of an 'Atlantic' and a 4-4-0 was often employed. Usually the 4-4-0 was the leading engine, but the 'Atlantic' occasionally acted as pilot on up trains, as in this mid 1920s scene at Crescent Junction, Peterborough. 'Atlantic' No. 4418 and 4-4-0 4312 are preparing to start a southbound train, under the watchful eye of the signalman.

This pair of pictures, depicting trains departing south from Grantham, tell very different stories, and indicate the variety of motive power and stock at work on the GN section in the mid 1920s.

Right above: Whilst a smartly attired official keeps a wary eye on the photographer, 'Pacific' No. 4473 Solario passes on March 26 1926, heading for King's Cross, with an express comprised of modern Gresley bogie stock. The train is signalled on the fast line, with the distant signal indicating a clear road ahead. No. 4473, named after the winner of the 1925 St Leger, was the first Gresley 'Pacific' to be withdrawn, and retained the GN type railed tender throughout its life.

Right, below: Reflecting an older era, Ivatt 'Atlantic' No. 4438 is leaking steam at the same location in charge of a rake of empty coaches of old, fixed-wheel stock and is taking the slow line out of the station. All the GNR 4-4-2s were built at Doncaster, No. 4438 being completed in 1908. Although the large 'Atlantics' were regarded as 'strong' engines when they first appeared, their performance was considerably improved when they were subsequently rebuilt with piston valves and 32-element superheaters. In this form they were capable of tackling all but the heaviest 'Pacific' turns.

Below: A double-headed express, bound for King's Cross, departs from Doncaster behind class D2 4-4-0 No. 4390, which is piloting a far from steam-tight Ivatt 'Atlantic'. Until the drive for economy decreed that they should be painted black, these 4-4-0s were shopped in lined green and No. 4390, built at Doncaster in 1903, appears to be in such pristine condition that it may well be in ex-works condition following overhaul. The second coach is a clerestory-roofed design dating from the early 1900s. As more Gresley coaches became available, older stock of this type was sent away or relegated to secondary duties.

Left: In this splendid array of GNR 'somersault' signals at Red Bank, just south of Doncaster, a down express is signalled to stop at the station, whilst Stirling 0-6-0ST No. 852 pauses awaiting the road. On the right is a train of old four-wheeled stock known as the 'Doncaster Dido', used for conveying works staff from the platform to Doncaster carriage works. Since any lateness of this train was reflected in lost time by those on board, any time lost greater than one minute had to be explained. The date of this scene is uncertain, but is probably circa 1920. The 0-6-0ST was later renumbered 3852 by the LNER.

The 'Silver Jubilee' at speed, with the distinctive 'A4' chime whistle sounding a melodious warning before entering the tunnel. The locomotive is one of the first four 'silver' A4 'Pacifics' with recessed drawgear and the name painted on the boiler cladding sheets. The 'Silver Jubilee' is seen here as a seven-coach train; in 1938 a further coach was added to the standard formation, but the schedule remained unaltered with a four-hour timing each way between King's Cross and Newcastle, with one stop.

The GC Section

Above: Marylebone, the GCR's London terminus, had seen few structural changes since it was opened in 1899 when this picture was taken on February 17 1928. The clusters of signs and advertisements were little changed from GCR days. Note the antique taxicabs and the well-known semi-circular bookstall, still in use today. Marylebone housed the LNER Board room, located at the front of the first floor of the terminal building.

Above: Great Central Railway Chief Mechanical Engineer from 1900 to 1922 was John G. Robinson who produced a series of locomotives which were not only robust, but often very elegant. Amongst his most renowned designs were the 'Atlantics' which were judged sufficiently well-proportioned to be nicknamed 'Jersey Lilies' after Lily Langtry, the celebrated Edwardian actress. GCR class 8 Nc. 1084 is pictured at Marylebone in 1912, in dark green GCR livery with the company's coat-of-arms adorning the splashers. GCR brunswick green was rather darker than the 'grass green' adopted by the LNER from the GNR, but both companies' engines featured black lining, edged in white, to accentuate the lines of their engines. Even the tops of the splashers were lined in GCR days. No. 1084 was renumbered 6084 by the LNER and reclassified 'C4'. The veteran bearded driver was Joshua Slowen, then enjoying retirement at the age of 82.

Another very succesful Robinson design was his 4-6-2T, intended for the outer suburban traffic from Marylebone. Pictured here is No. 168, which was built at the GCR works at Gorton, Manchester, in 1911. The GCR built 30 of these engines and in 1925/6 Gresley added to the class by ordering a further 13 from Hawthorn Leslie for service in the NE area, as no other tank engine design of similar power was available.

The Great Central's prestige trains ran between Marylebone and Manchester, a service which was maintained by the LNER. On certain trains the locomotive worked through from Neasden, the crew lodging overnight and returning with their engine the next day. In 1913 Robinson introduced a new class of 4-4-0 express engines which were amongst the most successful of their type ever built in Britain. As with other Robinson designs, the class was added to by Gresley, who in 1924 ordered a further 24 locomotives from outside contractors to meet an urgent demand for motive power in Scotland. Most of the original 1913 batch were named after Directors of the GCR, and this engine is LNER No. 5430 *Purdon Viccars*, Deputy Chairman of the Company until his death in 1918. The train consists of stock specially built for the Manchester service and is seen just north of Neasden. Apart from the LNER livery, this is a typically GCR scene. The class D11 'Large Director' type introduced in 1920 is represented in preservation by No. 506 *Butler Henderson*, preserved in working order on the Great Central Railway, Loughborough.

By 1930 the GCR coaches had been replaced on the most important trains by standard Gresley coaches with teak panelled sides and elliptical roofs. The elegant 'Atlantics' were painted black, with red lining, and suffered in comparison with the GN and NE 'Atlantics' which retained their green liveries. No. 5265 was based at Leicester and is seen heading the 6.20pm down Bradford express past Ruislip and Ickenham on the Great Western/Great Central joint line.

The GE Section

Right: Liverpool Street station, the main London terminus of the GE Section of the LNER, at 10.40am on a summer morning in 1925. The morning rush hour is over but passengers are still thronging the station, many having just arrived at platform 7 for a day's visit to the capital. Women's fashions have changed more than men's, but the headgear merits special attention! Behind the recently arrived B12 4-6-0 are a J69 0-6-0T and F5 and F4 2-4-2Ts, two of which are fitted with stovepipe chimneys, and trains consisting of close coupled four-wheeled six-a-side coaches working the 'Jazz' service on the Enfield and Chingford lines. These were shortly to be replaced by new trains of quintuple articulated coaches of Gresley design and N7 class 0-6-2Ts.

Left: Troops from the Somerset Light Infantry arrived at Liverpool Street's platform 10 from Colchester Barracks on August 8 1936 to take over guard duty at Buckingham Palace and other places in the capital from the Guards who were to be away training. Here we see the regimental band and advance guard. Servicemen of more recent vintage will notice that the band, under the bugle major, is formed up in fours. Note too the service dress of the period, with long puttees, blancoed belts and highly polished boots. The locomotive is of class B12/3, rebuilt to Gresley specifications from the GE design of 1911.

Right: At most important stations on the LNER, the Station Master's uniform included a silk hat. Here is H. C. R Calver, of Liverpool Street station, on November 27 1931, standing before a 'Sandringham' class 4-6-0 (right) and a B12 4-6-0. Mr Calver was in charge of staff of more than 400 people of all grades and was responsible for the efficient running of the station, and for the well being of the LNER's passengers. More than 200,000 passengers used Liverpool Street each day at the time of the Grouping, but this figure had fallen considerably by 1948 partly due to the diversion of the Loughton line and Fairlop loop services to the Central line of the London Underground.

Below: Liverpool Street was severely hit during the Second World War, and this scene in September 1940 on platform 2 shows blast damage to suburban carriages. On the platform are the remains of a coach bogie of Gresley pressed steel construction. Comparison of the vehicles in the LNER articulated set shows the relative comfort afforded to the first class passengers, as indicated by the width of panelling between the compartments. The first class seats had spring upholstery, but the third class seats were merely padded. The LMS station at Broad Street, at a higher level in the background, also suffered extensive damage to the retaining wall which separated the station from Sun Street passage. The track was extensively damaged and at least one open wagon has fallen into the passage.

Above: Liverpool Street was the first British railway station to be equipped with a self-service cafeteria. At the beginning of the fast food revolution, the opening of this facility on December 31 1947 was almost the last act of the LNER restaurateurs. Taking the first lunch here is the Hon. E. B. Butler Henderson, Chairman of the LNER Board's Hotels Committee, which was responsible for restaurants and restaurant cars.

Right: Fenchurch Street station was owned by the LNER but an increasing amount of its traffic originated on the LMS London, Tilbury and Southend line. From the Grouping until the outbreak of war the number of passengers using the station on weekdays increased from 50,000 to 70,000, necessitating a complicated remodelling of the station, carried out between 1932 and 1935 at a cost of £250,000. GE trains using the station included those to the dockside branches, and to Ilford and Ongar. In this 1924 view of the platform ends note the variety of signals on the bracket, including small calling-on arms giving indications to drivers when the main signals were out of their range of vision.

Left: There were six goods depots within ½-mile of Fenchurch Street; in the centre of the picture is the GNR Royal Mint Street Depot and beyond is the Midland Railway depot. The GER depot at Goodman's Yard is to the left, this being partly used as a bonded warehouse for wines and spirits imported through Harwich. All the depots were destroyed or badly damaged in the 1939-45 war. Four brake vans await duty outside the GN depot, still carrying pre-Grouping lettering. Two are of GN and two of GE origin: neither type was perpetuated by the LNER, whose standard 20-ton brake van was based on a NE design. The tank engine standing next to the water column appears to be a F4 2-4-2T, which is carrying the head-code for the Fenchurch Street-Woolwich (via Bromley) service.

Right: This photograph, taken in August 1923 before the Grouping had taken much effect, is very evocative of the erstwhile Great Eastern. Taken from Stratford Central signal box, looking towards London, the Channelsea curve is on the right, giving connections to the North London Railway at Victoria Park, and the Cambridge main line near Loughton Branch Junction. The signalbox was located at the back of platform 4, the mirror being provided to help the signalman, as his view east was obscured by the waiting room roof and chimney stacks. The N7 0-6-2T reflected in the mirror is one of those built at Stratford to A. J. Hill's design, whilst in the background a B12 4-6-0 and a tank engine — possibly a J69 0-6-0T — are keeping company with trains of very mixed empty stock.

Left: When LNER numbers were first allocated, and until the new company's transfers were available, Stratford followed the old GER practice of painting locomotive numbers in large characters on the tender sides, as illustrated here by 'Claud Hamilton' No. 8878 and J20 0-6-0 No. 8280. James Holden (GER Locomotive Superintendent, 1885-1907) had patented an oil burning system to supplement poor quality coal in locomotive fireboxes, and to utilise the oil waste from the gas producing plant at Stratford. This system was abandoned before the First World War, but a number of engines had the equipment reinstated during the coal strike of 1921. No. 8873 is having its bunker replenished at Stratford locomotive depot. The 'Clauds' dated from 1900, the pioneer engine of this capable class being named after GER Chairman Lord Claud Hamilton. The J20 was the most powerful 0-6-0 in Britain in its day, 25 having been built at Stratford in 1920-23; dimensionally they were as large as many eight-coupled classes.

Above: The most powerful express passenger engines handed on to the LNER by the GER were the '1500' class 4-6-0s, LNER class B12. The GER built 71 and a further 10 were obtained by the LNER from Beyer Peacock, of Manchester, during an acute motive power shortage in 1928. In this picture No. 8500, the first of the class, built at Stratford to S. D. Holden's design in 1911, is picking up water on the Ipswich water troughs, near Halifax Junction, south of Ipswich tunnel. The GER possessed only two-sets of troughs, the other being at Tivetshall.

Left: B12 4-6-0s occasionally appeared on the GC section in the early days of the Grouping, when their trains of Westinghouse air-braked stock helped out when there were heavy calls on rolling stock for such events as the Cup Final, at Wembley. No. 8507 is pictured in pristine condition at Wembley Hill with a special train from Nottingham carrying Boots employees to the British Empire Exhibition.

Above: A completely new train for the 'Hook Continental' service was built at York in 1938: the train featured luxurious accommodation and was finished in LNER varnished teak panelling at its splendid best. The boat express is seen here at Parkeston Quay. In charge of the train is No. 8517, one of the B12/3 class 4-6-0s modernised at Stratford with a range of modifications including a larger boiler and improved valve gear. Parkeston Quay was owned by the LNER, having originally been opened in 1883 and named after the GER Chairman of the day, Charles Henry Parkes.

Left : In the early days of the nationalised railways, LNER B1 4-6-0 No. 1236, built by the North British Locomotive Company in 1947, stands at the head of the inaugural 'Norfolkman' introduced on September 28 1948. A return trip to Norwich ran each day, leaving Liverpool Street at 10.00am. No. 1236's electric headlamps are supplemented here by the white circular discs used on the GE section. The B1 was the most numerous class constructed by the LNER: 410 examples entered service between 1942 and 1952, many being built after nationalisation in 1948. The class was originally intended as a mixed traffic type, but for a period they took charge of many important express passenger services on the GE section.

Facing page: The important Continental boat services from Parkeston Quay were provided with fast connecting trains from Liverpool Street, and a through train also ran from Liverpool and Manchester. New coaches of standard LNER design were provided for these trains soon after the Grouping. The locomotive here is B12 4-6-0 No. 8532, in LNER green livery and with polished brass rims to the splashers, arriving at Parkeston Quay in August 1927. On the right is the bay platform used by the local Parkeston Quay — Dovercourt Bay — Harwich service which remained a stronghold of six-wheeled carriages until the late 1930s. In the background is the Parkeston Quay Hotel, opened in 1884.

Right: Clearly inspired by the SR's famous poster, the original caption to this picture reads: 'Off for the school holidays. With the majority of schools for the summer holidays, railway stations are becoming thronged with eager and excited schoolchildren off for the long looked forward to summer holidays in the country or by the sea. Michael Fresco has a word with the engine driver before leaving Liverpool Street station, 23/7/55.'

The S. D. Holden B12 class were long-lived and remained popular with GE section crews until they were withdrawn at the end of the steam era. No. 61555 (rebuilt in 1935 as B12/3) is in charge of a Southend train about to leave Liverpool Street; the livery is BR black with the lining barely visible beneath the grime. The engine is still fitted with its Westinghouse pump, for working the locomotive brakes only, as all main stock was vacuum braked by this time. The 'RA4' on the cabside indicated the LNER route availability: in the case of the B12s the low number meant wide availability as a result of low axle loading. In contrast, Gresley's A4 'Pacifics' were 'RA9'. No. 61555 is in generally shabby condition and the leading 'mudhole' on the firebox top appears to be leaking badly.

Above left: London's East End seems to have had a four-year cycle of floods! On January 4 1928 Temple Mills goods yard, Stratford, was inundated, making the job of the shunter — never an easy task — even more difficult. No. 8176, recently superheated after working on saturated steam since construction at Stratford in 1901, was of class J17, the GER's freight equivalent of the 'Claud Hamilton' 4-4-0. The boiler and cylinder dimensions were similar, and the class had the commodious cab for which the GE was noted. For many years these engines provided the mainstay motive power for coal and heavy goods trains running between March and Temple Mills.

Above right: One of London's most severe thunderstorms broke at 2.30pm on August 1 1932, and flooding inevitably followed. The subway at Stratford station was impassable and arrangements were made to allow passengers to cross the running lines. All signals are at 'danger' as class F4 2-4-2T No. 7591 (built at Stratford in 1907) waits for permission to proceed with its train from Ilford to Fenchurch Street. The 2-4-2T was a popular type for GER suburban work, 172 engines being built in three classes between 1884 and 1912. By the Grouping, some of the older engines had been transferred to country districts in favour of more modern N7 0-6-2Ts. Only the platform at the extreme left remains today, the rest of the scene is virtually unrecognizeable. Note the miniature signal repeaters in front of the railwaymen at the base of the bracket signal.

Below: Heavy rains in Edmonton early in 1936 led to the closure of Silver Street on January 10, when the street was flooded to a depth of five feet. While the lorry driver on the far side of the bridge contemplates taking the plunge, N7 0-6-2T No. 8004 heads for Liverpool Street with a 10-coach train comprising two quintuple articulated sets. No. 8004 was built at Stratford in 1921 to the design of A. J. Hill, and this type was powerful for its size and with 4ft 10in driving wheels was noted for rapid acceleration. Where an adequate distance between stops permitted, the class was also capable of a fair turn of speed.

Above: This was the view on August 1 1932 during floods at Stratford station, where the Woolwich branch met the Colchester main line. The corrugated iron building in the centre background was the two-road shed used by the Stratford works shunters; the building beyond is the iron foundry. Today only the left-hand lines survive as part of the electrified 'North London' line between Stratford and Hackney.

Below & Below left: A short-lived strike by railway workers in 1919 led to restricted services and overcrowded suburban trains. Whilst no-one appears to have chanced travelling on a carriage roof, passengers seem to have risked their lives perched between the vehicles, or even sitting on the buffers — or were these scenes posed for photographer? Would a passenger really have travelled holding on to the gas lighting regulator lever, with one foot on the screw coupling? The pictures reveal interesting details of the coaches, which are four-wheeled panelled stock with six-a-side seating. The carriages had incandescent gas lighting and the smoking compartments had torpedo vents on the roof.

Above: The LNER's drive for economy resulted in a period of short-time working at Stratford works for some weeks in 1927. Two foremen are seen discussing the situation — note the bowler hat, an undisputed trademark of authority on the railways of this era, and the immaculately polished boots. The locomotives in the background are a J69 0-6-0T bearing the destination board 'Custom House' on its bunker back, and an N7 0-6-2T. The J69 class was used for both suburban passenger duties and for goods shunting work: the engines possesed detail differences according to the work they did.

Above: With the period of short-time working at an end, the Topical Press Agency despatched its photographer to produce a picture capturing the spirit of the return to full-time work. The uncredited photographer clearly went to some trouble to pose this picture, crouching in the coal with an unwieldy camera, probably for a lengthy time exposure, with the co-operation of the crew. The picture purports to show the crew preparing to take their engine out on the road again, apparently from the depths of the shed at Stratford.

The LNER purchased 56 4WVBT shunting engines manufactured by the Sentinel Waggon Works of Shrewsbury, the first trials being undertaken in 1925. These unusual locomotives were particularly useful for light work in yards where the track was of low standard, and they were based on the contemporary Sentinel steam road lorry, utilising a high-pressure vertical boiler. Some were used for work in the LNER's own yards, as illustrated here in the Sleeper Depot at Lowestoft. This is No. 8401, at first painted in plain black with small identification letters on the left-hand frame side. The regular stacks of sleepers are drying prior to creosoting; the wagons are GER sleeper wagons which featured largely open sides, though bottom side-planks were fitted to enable loads of spent ballast to be carried.

The NE Area

Right: A quiet moment at York station in June 1927. An up passenger train hauled by a North Eastern Railway 'Atlantic' is awaiting the signal to leave platform 4S whilst Scarborough shed's G5 0-4-4T No. 381 is in charge of a horse box on one of the centre roads, having just uncoupled from a local passenger working. The NER possessed three classes of 'Atlantic': 20 two-cylinder Class 'V' and 50 three-cylinder class 'Z' types, LNER classes C6 and C7 respectively. There were also two compound 4-4-2s of class '4CC', (LNER class C8). The NE 'Atlantics' worked the heaviest East Coast services between York and Edinburgh until they were replaced by 'Pacifics' in the years 1923-25. The G5 tank design numbered 110 engines, built at Darlington between 1894 and 1901, and were mainly used on suburban or branch line duties on all parts of the NER system.

Left: York's first station was built just inside the city walls, and the site was later used as carriage sidings before being abandoned altogether, to be replaced by a grassy bank and flower beds. This picture shows the station circa 1858, with the famous Minster in the background. York was the headquarters of the NER, and the NE Area of the LNER. The impressive station, office buildings and the Royal Station Hotel together represented a tribute to the solidarity of the erstwhile NER.

Below left: Two well-known features of the NER are impressively illustrated in this photograph of Newcastle Central station from the east, on November 13 1924. The complex multi-track crossing, with the East Coast Main Line on the lower right, and the rails (which converged to three tracks) to the High Level bridge on the left, utilised manganese steel castings to obtain long life, coupled with low maintenance. NER signalling practice was more elaborate than on most other railways and this gantry, with signals controlling entry and exit from the east end of the station, is typical of many others. Signals were worked by an electro-pneumatic system, one of the earliest of its kind to replace wholly manually worked installations.

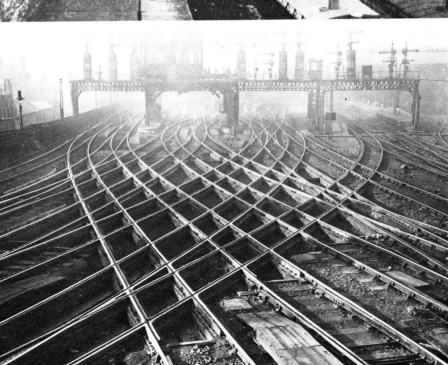

Left: The General Strike of May 1926 brought many volunteers to assist in maintaining rail services, and people in plain clothes were often seen in place of uniformed railwaymen. This was the situation during the strike at Wooden Gate Crossing, on the NE line between Newcastle and Berwick, where the volunteer guard has had to precede the train on foot, to open the level crossing gates. Waiting for a clear road is an LNER class D20 4-4-0, formerly a member of the celebrated NER 'R' class, 60 of which were built at Gateshead between 1899 and 1907. They were regular performers in pre-Great War days on what was then the fastest train in Britain, covering the 44¼ miles from Darlington to York in 43 minutes.

Right: The five 'Pacifics' built to the design of Sir Vincent Raven did not fit into any LNER standardisation programme, and when in 1929 No. 2404 *City of Ripon* needed a boiler overhaul, the LNER decided to fit one of the type designed for the Gresley 'Pacifics' rather than build a new one to the original specification. The Gresley boiler incorporated a wider firebox, necessitating the substitution of the high-window type of cab used on other Gresley designs, as a replacement for the original Darlington style. The modified engine is pictured here with G5 0-4-4T No. 529. Darlington works persisted for several years to display a degree of independence from LNER practice, indicated by the painting of 'Class 4-6-2' on the bufferbeam, six years after the Grouping, and when the class was officially designated as an 'A2'. Note that the connecting rod drives onto the leading coupled wheels, instead of the more conventional centre set.

Below right: The original track of the Stockton & Darlington Railway crossed the East Coast Main Line on the level just north of the present Darlington Bank Top station. Making a vigorous approach to the crossing during 1925 is NER class 'Z' 4-4-2 (LNER class C7) No. 727, with an express bound for Newcastle. This class was introduced by NER Chief Mechanical Engineer V. L. Raven (later Sir Vincent Raven) in 1911 as the first three-cylinder express passenger class to be built in Britain. Unlike Gresley, who chose to actuate the inside cylinder valves by conjugated gear derived from the outside motion, Raven preferred to use independent gear for each set of valves, which led to congestion between the frames, compared with Gresley's engines.

Left: The fireman watches the photographer as his engine, 'Z' class 'Atlantic' No. 2210, heads south near Harrogate with an up Pullman working of five vehicles. No. 2210, allocated to Heaton shed, Newcastle, is working through to Leeds where the train would be strengthened by coaches from Bradford and worked forward to London probably by one of the Ivatt 'Atlantics' specially selected for the Pullman link.

Below: The first of the LNER D49 Class 4-4-0s, No. 234 *Yorkshire* heads a ten-vehicle restaurant car express of mixed composition. The restaurant car (the second carriage in the train) is of NER origin with an inverted bow-string type underframe, as used also on the East Coast Royal Saloons. The 'D49s' were introduced in 1927 for service in the North East and Scotland: the first batches utilised conventional piston valves and were named after Shires, but Gresley later decided to adopt Lentz poppet valves and the engines thus modified were named after Hunts. Sole surviving D49 is No. 246 *Morayshire* (BR No. 62712), built in 1928.

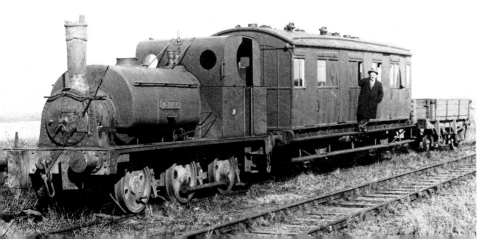

Left: Not strictly LNER, but certainly of associated interest was the little-known military line which linked Kilnsea to Spurn Head. This railway was not connected to the LNER system, and was operated by the Royal Engineers. This picture, taken after closure of the line, depicts an ancient 0-6-0ST, converted into a 2-4-0 by removal of the leading coupling rods, and named *Kenyon*. LNER class Y8 0-4-0T No. 559 was taken to the line by low-loader in 1940 and worked there for about a year.

Edinburgh Waverley

Right: Waverley station, Edinburgh, was one of the largest stations on the LNER system, its position being dominated by the imposing bulk of the North British Hotel, topped by its well-known clock tower. In this view, D11 'Director' 4-4-0 No. 6388 *Captain Craigengelt* is pulling out of the west end of the station. This locomotive was one of a series built in 1924 specially for service in Scotland and the batch were named after characters in Sir Walter Scott's literary works. Gresley's emerging influence at this time is indicated by the four-compartment brake third coach behind the tender and the N2 0-6-2T just visible above its roof in the background. Several 'N2s' were built for service north of the border.

Passing through Princes Street Gardens and entering Waverley from the west is the 'Queen of Scots' Pullman, which originated in Glasgow and continued on to King's Cross via Harrogate and Leeds. The engine in charge is No. 9877 *Liddesdale*, one of the robust 'Atlantics' built by W. P. Reid for the heaviest North British services. A total of 22 of these powerful-looking locomotives were built between 1906 and 1921 and at the Grouping, such was the shortage of motive power in Scotland that the NB operating authorities asked for five more. In the event, the demand was met by the allocation of five of Gresley's new 'Pacifics'.

The Forth Bridge

Above: A contemporary illustration of the Forth Bridge at the time of its opening on March 4 1890.

Above right: A living model depicting the cantilever principle used in the Forth Bridge.

THE FORTH BRIDGE COMPANY was formed in 1861, the North British Railway agreeing to contribute 35% of the cost of the bridge, with 30% coming from the Midland Railway, and 17½% each from the North Eastern and Great Northern Railways. Thus, at the Grouping the bridge was owned jointly by the LNER, which had a majority interest, and the LMS. The engineers were John Fowler and Benjamin Baker and the contractor was William Arrol — who also built London's Tower Bridge over the Thames. The structure was based on the cantilever principle, as demonstrated by the illustration of the three men in which two, with arms outstretched, can support the third between them, their chains being kept in equilibrium by anchorages at each end.

The bridge consisted of three massive diamond-shaped towers, built slowly until they reached 341ft above the high water level; the towers were anchored to masonry structures at each, providing the road-bed for the approaching rails, and finally the two central linking sections were completed by being built outwards from each cantilever arm. Construction of the bridge went on day and night, throughout the year, workmen operating in two 12-hour shifts. There were 57 fatalities and 500 men were seriously injured before the bridge was opened in March 1890 by the Prince of Wales, later Edward VII. Most fatalities and injuries were caused by men falling, or resulted from rivets and pieces of metal being dropped onto workers beneath.

The Forth Bridge represented a major advance in contemporary construction techniques and it was completed not long before the Eiffel Tower, with which it was favourably compared. Steel sections were cut and shaped at an extensive workshop specially constructed on the Queensferry side of the Forth, and these were delivered as required to the erectors, who rivetted them into place. No scaffolding was needed: a circular cage was built which surrounded the main tubular members, this moving along as the tubes grew. Steam cranes were employed to raise material to site, and lifts provided for the workmen.

Above: One of the partly completed main piers of the Forth Bridge, viewed from the north bank in July 1888.

Including approaches, the Bridge is 1½-miles long and its construction required 54,000 tons of steel and 640,000 cubic feet of granite, brought from Aberdeen. It took eight years to complete (three years longer than Ribblehead Viaduct, on the Settle-Carlisle line) but it was time well-spent, for the structure has carried East Coast trains of increasing weight for almost 100 years, with complete success.

Above: With the main piers virtually complete, work is commencing on the central suspended section of the bridge, by working outward from each cantilever. This picture depicts progress on the Bridge in April 1889.

Right: Rivetting in hand on the Garvie pier, using the circular 'cages' which were moved along the cylindrical spars as construction advanced.

No. 10000 — Gresley's 'Hush-Hush'

Above: The Glasgow firm of Yarrow & Co. had specialised in the manufacture of water-tube boilers for marine use, and in association with Sir Harold Yarrow, Gresley developed No. 10000, a 4-6-4 locomotive with a 450psi boiler and four-cylinder compound operation. The locomotive, illustrated in ex-works condition, was constructed over a number of years in conditions of such secrecy that it was dubbed the 'Hush-Hush'. Its unconventional engineering features were hidden beneath an all-over sheet steel covering: it was painted in dark grey livery, relieved only by the polished steel bands around the boiler cladding. The locomotive entered service in 1930 and was the subject of numerous trials and modifications. It worked for a time on top link duties from Gateshead, as well as a round trip on the non-stop 'Flying Scotsman'. The 'Hush-Hush' was regarded as a prestige locomotive by the LNER and it was a frequent visitor to many of the exhibitions held throughout the company's system in the early 1930s. The locomotive, the first 4-6-4 tender engine built for use in Britain, had 6ft 8in diameter wheels and an overall weight in working order (including the tender) of 166 tons.

Left: The front view of No. 10000 was radically different from anything before seen in Britain. With the partially obscured smokebox door and curved side sheet, two ducts from above the buffers to behind the chimney were all designed to help lift the exhaust clear of the locomotive, to prevent the driver's forward vision being obscured. Lessons learned from the shape of the sheet-steel casing were put to good effect in later designs like *Cock o' the North* and the streamlined 'Pacifics'. The front end shape was finalised following detailed wind tunnel experiments with a wooden model, in which air was passed through the tunnel at about 50mph and powdered chalk projected through the chimney.

Right: No. 10000's cab layout was a new departure for LNER footplatemen. The end of the main steam drum, set high in the cab, prevented the normal positioning of the steam manifold, and this was mounted immediately above the firehole door. The main regulator handle (visible in the driver's spectacle window) admitted HP steam to the HP steam chests, but to facilitate starting a second regulator admitted live steam to the LP steam chests: this supply had to be shut off as soon as the engine was under way. The small levers on the cab floor to the right of the driving seat operated the HP and LP reversing gear.

Below: In its early years, No. 10000 was stationed at Gateshead and often visited Edinburgh on trains normally worked by Gresley 'Pacifics'. The only known occasion it crossed the Forth Bridge was February 23 1930, when it worked a trial train to Perth and back. The instruments on the side of the locomotive were for recording steam pressure and providing information on the performance of the 'Hush-Hush', in conjunction with the LNER dynamometer car coupled behind the tender. The train was stationary when the photograph was taken, a 'photo-stop' having been specially arranged.

Right: Two men are turning No. 10000 by hand at King's Cross station yard as a cameraman films the operation with a hand-cranked camera — both operations to be mechanised before long at this time. Note the additional handrail in front of the smokebox, added after the locomotive had been in service for a year. The unconventional appearance of the 'Hush-Hush' is clearly apparent in this view, and its impact on the railwaymen, observers and passengers of the era can be easily imagined. A rather more down-to-earth 'N2' hurries past in the background, having left the King's Cross suburban platforms with a train of articulated Gresley stock.

Left: At King's Cross, No. 10000 keeps company with what the original photographer's caption describes as an 'ordinary type of engine' — the aim was obviously to highlight the modern approach of the 'Hush-Hush'. The 'ordinary' engine is in fact No. 2576 *The White Knight*, one of two Gresley 'Pacifics' to be fitted with French ACFI boiler feedwater heating apparatus. This equipment, mounted on the running plate, heated feedwater with exhaust steam and while some savings were made in both coal and water, it was found that extra maintenance costs more than outweighed the benefits and the apparatus was removed in 1938. It certainly detracted from the otherwise sleek lines of the class. The other locomotive modified in this way was No. 2580 *Shotover*, which was also one of the first Gresley 'Pacifics' to be fitted with a 220psi boiler and thus reclassified from 'A1' to 'A3.' Both were based on the North East and were not often seen in London, although prior to modification with the ACFI equipment, *Shotover* had worked the inaugural up non-stop 'Flying Scotsman' from Edinburgh on May 1 1918, whilst on loan to Haymarket shed.

Below left: Whilst many lessons were learned from experience with the 'Hush-Hush' it was too unreliable in its original condition to take its place in everyday running. Consequently in 1937 it was rebuilt in simple form with a 250psi boiler, and given the overall stream-lined outline of the 'A4s', though it retained its 4-6-4 wheel arrangement. With its 20in x 26in cylinders, No. 10000 was the most powerful 6ft 8in-wheeled locomotive to be built in Britain, but although it was fitted with a corridor tender it was never regularly used on the non-stop 'Flying Scotsman'. The locomotive is seen here entering King's Cross from Doncaster, with its first working after rebuilding, on November 14 1937.

Electric traction

Right: In the mid-1930s the Government made money available to the LNER at a low rate of interest, £1.6 million of which was allocated to the electrification of the cross-Pennine line between Manchester and Sheffield, together with the mineral branch to Wath. One of the last two of Gresley's designs (the other being the small V4 class 2-6-2) was a powerful mixed traffic electric locomotive, numbered 6701 and built in 1940 as the first of a numerous class designed specially for the MS&W route. The supply system was 1,500 volts DC overhead and the locomotive was constructed at Doncaster the electrical machinery being supplied by Metropolitan Vickers. The lettering was a mixture of traditional block characters on the body sides, with the lozenge-shaped LNER logo containing 'Gill Sans' lettering on each door. No. 6701 weighed 87 tons and had a one-hour rating of 1,870hp; its maximum speed was 65mph, and with a 750-ton train the running time compared with steam traction would be reduced from 162 to 97 minutes. No. 6701 ran on the Netherlands railway system between 1947 and 1952 whilst work on the MS&W electrification, held up during the war, was completed. A total of 57 further locomotives were built to this general design, which provided the backbone of motive power on the Woodhead route until it closed in 1981. Note No.6701's standard LNER oval worksplate and bogie-mounted drawgear, in contrast to the normal practice of securing the drawbar to the locomotive body.

Thirteen electric locomotives entered LNER service, in three classes. The largest was intended to be the prototype of a main line passenger class to be used on the electrified NE line between York and Newcastle which in the event did not proceed. The others were Bo-Bos, ten larger locomotives being employed on the Shildon-Newport mineral line, and two smaller examples on the short, steeply graded Newcastle Quayside branch. This had been electrified as early as 1905, using a 600 volt. DC overhead system of supply. The two locomotives were numbered NER 1 and 2, these numbers being retained in LNER days. In this picture No.2, still in NER livery in 1924, is seen by the main line between Manors and Heaton, opposite Argyle Street signal box. Also in the picture is J71 0-6-0T No. 572,, then 33 years old and which continued in service until 1961, when it was retired after a working life of 69 years.

Above: 6701's driver has his right hand on the 'notching plate,' cutting out sections of field resistance as the locomotive gathers speed, watching both the ammeter and the track ahead. Other controls include a 'weight transfer' switch, which allowed for weakening the field of the leading motor of each bogie, so that maximum tractive effort could be obtained from the rear bogie motors when starting a heavy load. This was because at starting the locomotive tended to 'sit-down' on its rear bogie, thus increasing the possibility of wheelslip on the leading bogie. The driver normally stood at his console, with his foot on the deadman's pedal. The driver's left hand is on the vacuum brake valve, for applying the continuous train brake; the duplex gauge showing 21in of vacuum in both the train pipe and vacuum chamber is immediately behind the brake valve. The handle to the right of the 'notching' plate is marked' 'forward and reverse.' Note the 'LMS & LNE' lettering on the driver's collar.

Left: A 300kW Bastian & Athen immersion heated boiler was provided for working the carriage steam heating systems and the steam locomotive-style boiler gauge glass for this equipment is visible on the right.

Above: A fine detailed view of the electrical switchgear equipment fitted to No. 6701. It was impossible to get into this room until both pantographs had been lowered, this releasing the electrical door lock. It is believed that the household-type electricity meter secured to the wall was used to record energy consumption whilst the locomotive ran trials on the Altrincham line, this enabling the LMS to charge the LNER for electricity consumed! The looped cables certainly indicate a temporary connection.

Above: Regenerative braking was an important aspect of No. 6701's design and operation. In this system a motor generator set is switched into circuit at the beginning of the descent, electricity being generated and fed back into the overhead supply conductor through the pantograph, whilst at the same time a mechanical resistance was set up to retard movement of the train. The steep inclines on both sides of Woodhead tunnel enabled this locomotive and its successors to make full use of these Metropolitan Vickers motor-generator sets.

Passenger stock & train catering

Right: New Coaches were provided for the 'Flying Scotsman' train in 1928, when non-stop running between London and Edinburgh was introduced, and particular attention was paid to the internal decor. Sir Charles Allom was commissioned to advise on the first class restaurant cars, which departed from traditional British coach interiors by being furnished in Louis XIV style. As shown in this picture this featured loose chairs, concealed lighting and matching wall colourings and curtains. In those days, ladies took luncheon wearing their hats!

Above: Gresley's coaches were solidly built with teak panelling and framing, and many lasted well into BR days. This example, BR No. 13369E, pictured on May 7 1952, was built at Doncaster in 1935 as an open third class carriage, and converted into a cafeteria car in 1952 as part of the popular trend towards self-service meals. Many Gresley buffet cars were also refurnished and given a new lease of life by the new owners. However, the varnished teak finish of the LNER stock did not take kindly to the sprayed maroon and cream of the new livery and the repainted coaches sometimes took on a rather unkempt appearance as a result.

Left: An apple for the fireman on July 13 1938. Sir Nigel Gresley once said that the smallest vehicle he had been called upon to design was a platform refreshment trolley. This is unlikely to have been the one shown here, which in its mechanical features bears more than a passing resemblance to the supermarket trolley of today, and was probably just as difficult to steer! This was a new service introduced by the LNER in 1938 at both King's Cross and Liverpool Street stations, and these smartly uniformed girls served passengers in their trains prior to departure. Apples and pears are 2d each (less than 1p), or for the same price you could sample a packet of Smith's crisps — each containing the famous blue 'twist' of salt! A brimming box of fruit is priced at 1/6 and bunches of bananas at 1/- The engine is Ivatt 'Atlantic' No. 4400, then stationed at New England, Peterborough, and the train is probably the 11.30am stopping service for York.

Above: Another view of the platform refreshments service launched at King's Cross in the summer of 1938. Of interest is 'N2' 0-6-2T No. 2681, waiting to leave with the empty coaches of a recently-arrived express. The smartly turned-out restaurant car has in one of its windows the circular 'Smoking prohibited' sign of the day.

Left: The smartly uniformed salesgirl, who was probably a model hired for the photographic session, also offered a selection of fruit from a tray. This is an attractive and interesting picture, though one cannot help wondering if this service really would have been welcomed by the passengers — or the staff for that matter — of this Pullman Car train?

An early experiment in on-train entertainment by the LNER was this cinema coach, photographed here at King's Cross on February 13 1924. The vehicle was converted from a GNR saloon and the film on offer is 'Black Oxen,' starring Corinne Griffith, a star of the silent screen of the era. This particular film is not regarded today as a classic — one wonders how the passengers of 1924 reacted to this service. The coach is parked in platform 10 at King's Cross, but whether it was actually marshalled in the 'Flying Scotsman' itself at the time is less certain.

Left: An interesting experiment took place on May 20 1932 when wireless telephone communication was tried between the 'Flying Scotsman' train and an Imperial Airways aeroplane. The aircraft 'Hercules', carrying 38 passengers and a crew of three, was on its way to Glasgow for the Scottish Flying Club's pageant. Leaving Croydon airport at 11am it caught up with the 'Flying Scotsman' between Grantham and Doncaster and messages were exchanged between passengers. To help the pilot identify the train, the 'Flying Scotsman' name was displayed in large letters on the roof of the last coach, which was fitted with a Marconi aircraft wireless set for the occasion. Note the sinuous path taken by the train from platform 7 to the mouth of Gas Works tunnel.

Below left: 'Talkies' eventually made their way into the LNER's trains in 1935 when a standard bogie brake van was converted into a 44-seat cinema coach, complete with sloping floor and back-projection screen. The grandly titled 'LNER-Pathe Cinema Car,' usually offered a 1-hour show consisting of news and general interest items, for which one shilling entry fee was charged. This picture was taken on May 24 1935 and the 'Today's Film Programme' display behind the attendant lists the Jubilee Celebrations, Pathe News and Sport to entice the passenger. The Car worked to Leeds on the 10.10am from King's Cross, returning at 3.30pm, staffed by an LNER attendant who collected tickets, and a Pathe employee to operate the cinema equipment. The coach was very successful and the following year a second brake van was similarly converted for use between Leeds and Glasgow. Both cars reverted to use as ordinary brake vans soon after the outbreak of war on September 3 1939.

The introduction of the camping coach was an interesting innovation in 1933. An old passenger carriage would be parked in a country siding — this one was at Bowes, Yorkshire — after conversion to provide family living accommodation for 6 people. This vehicle was GNR six-wheeled six compartment carriage No. 42210, pictured in its new guise on August 1 1933. Providing rail fares to the local station were paid, the coach cost £2.10.0 per week in the summer, or £2 in off-peak weeks.

Right: Senior officials used a special coach when out on tours of inspection, sometimes hauled by an elderly locomotive reserved specially for the purpose. In this scene, photographed in August 1925, a special is being worked by NER 2-4-0 No. 1466 (LNER class E5) known on the North Eastern as 'class 1463' after the class pioneer, built in 1885. No. 1466 is smartly turned-out in LNER green, but this was very much an 'Indian summer' for the engine was withdrawn in January 1927. The coach is an old NER saloon, and the train has stopped on the line between Shildon and Erimus Yard, Newport. This route was electrified in 1915 and operated by ten 1,100hp double-bogie locomotives, which worked coal from pits in Co.Durham to Teeside for export or the steelworks. However, with the slump in coal exports in the 1920s, traffic declined to such an extent that the line reverted to steam traction in 1935.

Left: This 1938 bogie camping coach was rather more commodious than the older six-wheeled vehicle illustrated on p 55. Camping coach No. CC66 was a former East Coast Joint Stock vehicle with matchboarded sides, originally built by the NER and painted in a cheerful green and white for its new role. The carriage is on display here at Marylebone's platform 4, a venue frequently used for the display of new rolling stock to the press and public, before making a week's tour of the Yorkshire Dales.

Right: In 1928 both the LMS and the LNER introduced third class sleeping coaches on the Anglo-Scottish overnight services. Berths, pillows and blankets were provided for four people, but no sheets, and toilet facilities were available at the end of the corridor. Men and women were normally segregated, although exceptions were made for families. The LNER management were initially concerned that business might be diverted from the first class sleeping cars, but this proved unfounded as first class cars provided a higher standard of comfort and catered for one person, with washing facilities included in the compartment. The LNER cars featured blankets boldly emblazoned 'LNER KING'S CROSS'.

The sleeping cars, which actually entered service on September 24, consisted of ordinary third class corridor coaches with seven compartments, each having hinged beds on each wall to form upper berths; each compartment thus accomodating four people on overnight runs. The coaches were capable of being used on ordinary services in daylight hours. The third class sleeping cars were introduced between King's Cross and Edinburgh: the LMS and GWR also introduced similar facilities at this time.

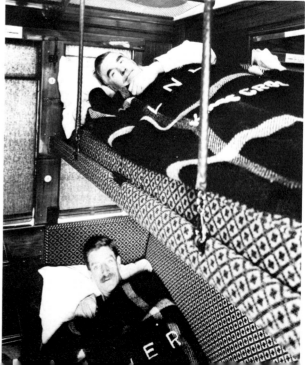

Above: New trains were provided for the non-stop 'Flying Scotsman' in 1938, and for the 'Sunday Scotsman' services operated that year in connection with the Scottish Empire Exhibition in Glasgow, Each train included a buffet lounge coach of a new design: the normal Gresley corridor coaches were 61ft 6in in length but the new carriages were 5ft longer. On April 26 1938 one of the new buffet lounge cars is under construction in the body shop at Doncaster Carriage works. The steel under-frame was fabricated at York whilst Doncaster assembled the floor, sides, ends, roof, interior partitions and furnishings. One of the buffers carries the works code 'CME.842 CN.94 BUF-FET LOUNGE' while a notice hung in the roof girders proclaims:' Stage 1: Assemble & bolt floor to frame. Erect body ends and side quarters, Fix cant rails & panels. Body, 1 coat of Gold size.'

Left: A first/third composite coach was also included in the composition of each of the 'Flying Scotsman' trains, one of which ran down to Edinburgh whilst the other ran in the opposite direction. Also on April 26 1938 welders are at work on one of these composite carriages at Doncaster, assembling the brackets to carry the batteries. The body is largely complete. These trains represented the best of conventional teak panelled design, with pressure ventilation and double-glazed windows.

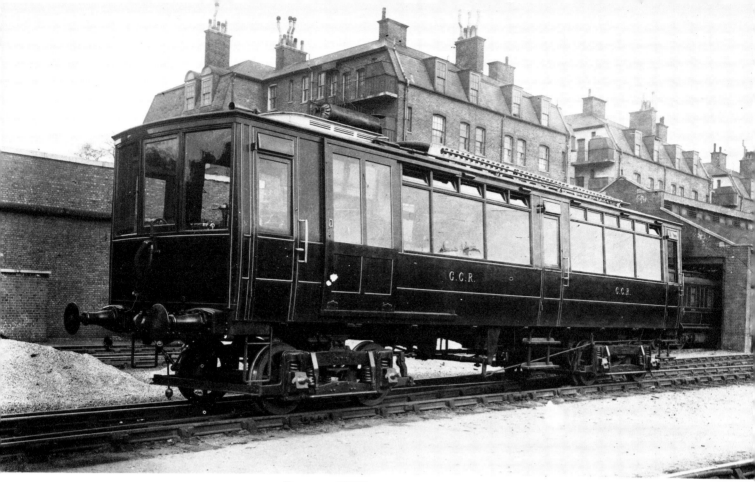

This was one of the Great Central Railway's attempts to tackle the problem of relatively little-used branch line services. In the early 1900s these duties had frequently been operated by auto-trains, in which a small locomotive and one or two coaches shuttled back and forth along a branch line, the engine remaining at one end and provision made for driving from a special compartment at the opposite end of the train. In the search for greater economies several railway companies experimented with railcars in which a small steam engine was contained within the body of the carriage. The GCR went one step further in 1912 with this railcar, which featured petrol-electric transmission: it was said to have been built after the GCR General Manager Sir Sam Fay had seen a similar vehicle at work in Hungary a couple of years previously.

Built by the Westinghouse Electric & Manufacturing Co.Ltd, the railcar was powered by a six-cylinder 90 hp four-stroke petrol engine designed to run at around 950rpm; it was also fitted with a governor to stop the engine racing should the load suddenly be thrown off. The engine drove a shunt-wound 55kW generator through a flexible coupling, energy then being supplied to two motors rated at 64hp each. These were fitted to the axles of the rear bogie, in order to balance the weight of the engine and generator at the other end of the vehicle, in a special compartment behind the leading driving cab.

The railcar, which had a range of 200 miles, carried out an inaugural trip from Marylebone to South Harrow on March 28 1912, carrying a party of VIPs including GCR Electrical Engineer C.W.Neele. The maximum speed,

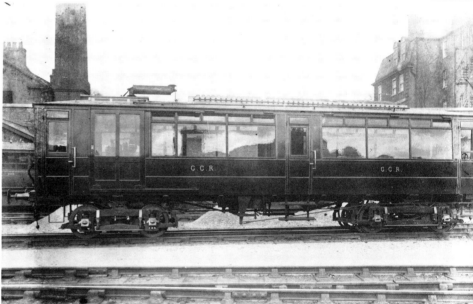

Top & above: These views, taken at Marylebone carriage sidings in 1912, illustrate the vehicle's construction details, and the light, airy nature of the railcar. The GCR painted teak livery was lined in gold. The central door gave access to the two passenger compartments.

attainable on the level, of 40mph was achieved during this run. The vehicle worked on this route for many years, being transferred north in 1919 to work on the Glossop branch: it then moved again in 1921 to run on the short branch between Bollington and Macclesfield on the GC and North Staffordshire joint line, where it was known as 'the Bollington Bug.' The railcar had a comparatively long life, not being withdrawn until 1935, after 23 years at work, when it was replaced by LNER 'Sentinel' railcars, notably No. 43301 *Commerce*.

Right: The interior of the car revealed the influence of American practice, with 'throw-over' seat backs, adjustable to the direction of travel. The decor was of oak and American ash with a natural grain finish, with a wooden slatted floor. The interior was electrically lit by a secondary, smaller generator powered by the engine, there were seats for 50 people, though emergency seats could be fitted if required, and straps were provided for standing passengers. The overall inside headroom was 7ft 6in, while, the vehicle was 41ft 6in long over headstocks and 8ft 6in wide.

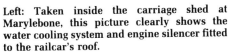

Left: Taken inside the carriage shed at Marylebone, this picture clearly shows the water cooling system and engine silencer fitted to the railcar's roof.

Below left:
The engine compartment, with access door open, also showing the driving compartment, the controls of which included a 'dead man's handle.' The driver controlled the vehicle from a standing position. Vacuum brakes were operated by a small exhauster powered by the petrol engine.

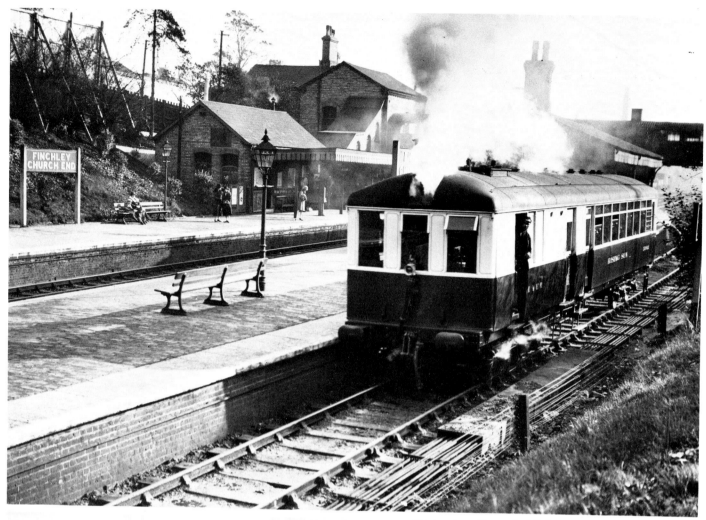

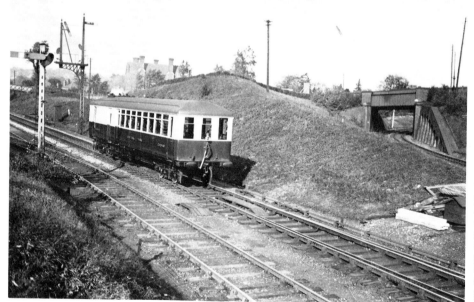

With the engine compartment furthest from the camera. *Rising Sun* approaches the High Barnet line junction, signalled for the branch platform. Described in the news photographer's original caption as 'London's first Tram-Trains' these railcars had capacity for 64 people and the passenger compartment was fitted with bi-directional seating with reversible backs. The cars were electrically lit and steam heated and had enough coal to give a 200-mile range, though the water capacity was sufficient for just 50 miles. The cars were capable of a top speed of 55mph.

Above: A delightful scene in sunny weather at Finchley Church End on October 29 1929 as Sentinel steam railcar No. 51912 *Rising Sun* leaves the branch platform with a working to Edgware. This unit operated this service from August 1929 to September 1930 including, for a time, one journey to High Barnet and back on weekdays. It was later transferred to Hitchin.

The LNER championed the use of self-contained steam railcars between the wars and nearly 90 were acquired between 1925 and 1930 from two manufacturers; Sentinel and the Clayton Wagon Company. The railcars were bought as part of the LNER's determination to reduce branch line running costs but while they coped well with the normal light traffic on these routes, they were too small to meet demand on busier market days and their lightweight construction led to a lack of mechanical reliability. The railcars were painted green and cream and named after well known stage coaches of bygone years: *Trafalgar*, *British Queen*, *Royal Sovereign* and *True Briton* being particularly inspiring examples. *Rising Sun* was driven by a 100hp six-cylinder engine coupled to a vertical high-pressure boiler similar to those used by the Sentinel company in its famous road lorries of the era. The engine and powered bogie were pivoted within a rigid body whereas earlier types had been powered by two-cylinders with the engine compartment and power bogie being articulated to the passenger compartment.

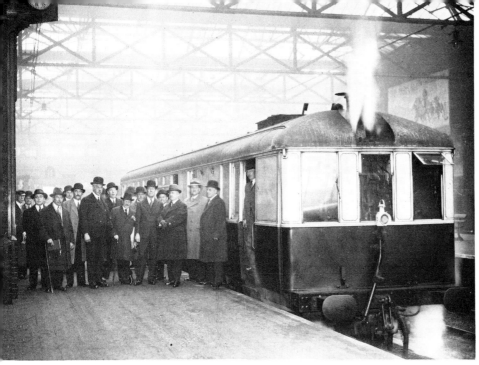

Left: The steam railcar manufacturers were anxious to obtain export orders for their vehicles on the strength of the LNER experience. A delegation from Roumania, led by General Mihail Jonescu, Director-General of the Roumanian State Railways is seen with H.N. Gresley (seventh from the left) and Sir Ralph Wedgwood (fifth from the right) on platform 11 at King's Cross on November 9 1931. The party travelled on a special trip to Hatfield, aboard No. 51914 *Royal Forester*. The enamel advertisement on the station wall promotes' Veno's Lightning Cough Cure for coughs, colds, flue and bronchial asthma!'

Above: The rival Clayton Wagon Company railcars, (11 were built for the LNER) as illustrated here by No. 2130 *Bang Up* were less attractive and less successful than their Sentinel Cammell counterparts. The Clayton vehicles were easily identified by the unsightly external coal bunker and spoked coupled wheels on the power bogie. Metropolitan Cammell also supplied coach-work for *Bang Up*, which started running trials in 1928, between Lincoln and Woodhall, where it is pictured prior to transfer to Hitchin for service to Hertford North. The railcar was retained for nearly two years on this duty before being replaced by Sentinel railcar No. 51909 *Waterloo*, after which it was moved to the GE section to work between Norwich and Lowestoft.

Left: The rear of *Bang Up*, which also accommodated 64 passengers, was rather more similar to the Sentinel cars. The original number 2130 was changed to 44 and later changed again to 43304; the vehicle was withdrawn in January 1937, principally because the manufacturer was no longer in business.

The **LNER** dynamometer car

recalled by D. R. CARLING.

I WORKED in the dynamometer car office of the LNER at Darlington for much of the 1937-39 period as Test Inspector under Tom Robson, the Chief Test Inspector, and succeeded him as such in 1946. We continued test programmes with the car until the 1948 locomotive exchange trials, though by this time I was mainly concerned with the Locomotive Testing Station at Rugby, where I was appointed Superintending Engineer.

The first dynamometer car tests in which I took part were those of 'B17' 4-6-0 No. 2861. This involved controlled testing at constant speeds and cut-offs using the counter-pressure locomotive, 'B13' No. 761 (later No.1699) as a brake. Mr Robson was usually at the recording table noting down observations from the lab as they came over the intercom. Christopher Jarvis, the Senior Test Inspector, would be noting the readings of the temperatures of inlet and exhaust steam and smokebox gases every two minutes, while Percy Dobson, the next senior man, was on the brake locomotive. I would be marking the record, using a bell-push to record mile posts, gradient boards, and stations or noting the water level in the tender. Barlow, normally a materials inspector, was on the B17 and a pupil or apprentice from North Road works was temporarily added to the crew. There was also Charlie Trewitt, the dynamometer car attendant, who generally looked after the car but who was also a qualified guard and acted as such if no regular guard was available.

These tests occupied four days in each of two weeks. For the first week it was sufficient to run from Darlington to York and back, but for the second week a preliminary run was made for the test to start at Eaglescliffe and on the return trip from York out to Church Fenton, this being to get the test engine thoroughly warmed up before actual testing began. When testing was complete all observations had to be evaluated and the material prepared for presentation as a report: this took a good deal longer than the actual testing, a principle which also applied to the preparation and planning which had to take place before a test. In this instance there were more than 300 observations of each of seven variable quantites, as well as about 350ft of record roll to be examined and measured to evaluate the individual elements of time, and work done from which better figures of speed and power were calculated, graphs plotted and other conclusions drawn.

In bitterly cold weather I recall some tests being done to analyse the amount of steam needed for train heating; for simplicity this was done with a stationary train at York, to which the car was coupled, but before tests could start we had to defrost the heating equipment coach by coach, using blowlamps to thaw the drip valves and the swan-neck fittings leading to the flexible coupling hoses. At the start of the test, the flow meter in the car went right up to the end-stop at more than 2,000 lb/hour, where it stayed for nearly half an hour before dropping back to something under 1,000 lb, but even so it was more than an hour before the twelfth coach began to be tolerably warm.

The next set of tests were made to obtain data for the impending electrification of the Manchester-Sheffield line, not so much to check the

Above: The 1906 NER dynamometer car during preparations for a test involving NER 'Atlantic' No. 706. The test car crew are taking cables forward over the tender to establish intercom communication between the cab and the recording table. The compartment at the rear of the car housed a small workshop, a cooking stove and a bed for the dynamometer car attendant in case the car was away overnight. There was also a WC compartment. In later years the NER bogies were replaced by Gresley bogies to improve high-speed running and a gangway connection was added at each end for access to the train or the locomotive, when a corridor tender was involved. The windows nearest the leading end were also later replaced by ex-guard's van window 'blisters' to give a forward view around the tender.

existing locomotive's performance, but more to assess what the electric locomotives would be required to do. Whilst measuring the pull required to start a heavy coal train out of some sidings the measuring wheel dropped off the rail, because of the very sharp curvature of the track, and it was only lifted back just in time to prevent serious damage when the rails straightened: luckily the two 2-8-0s hauling the train were only moving at walking pace.

Whilst the test car was carrying out work like this, well away from base, we had to stay in rooms, or at a hotel and when so doing I have stayed in hotels in Edinburgh, Leeds, London, Manchester, Newcastle and Yarmouth on the LNER and later at Inverness, Newport and Perth in BR days, and at hostels at Perth and Old Oak Common. During most tests there was a sufficient interval for a mid-day meal to be eaten in peace and the dynamometer car's galley could supply plenty of tea — only once do I recall that drinking water ran out on a long test in exceptionally hot weather. Occasionally it could be quite a problem to attend to the needs of the inner man on some tests.

In mid 1938 the dynamometer car was used in connection with the brake trials, some coaches from one of the 'Coronation' train sets having been fitted with a new type of quick service application brake valves. The car's function was to measure the time and distance required to stop from the moment the driver's brake valve was moved, this being marked on the record. For greater accuracy the paper speed of 2ft per mile was used. The individual brake events were separately recorded in one of the train coaches. A number of stops were made from high speeds on the down journey from King's Cross to Grantham, and on the up journey A4 'Pacific' *Mallard* recorded its world speed record burst at 126mph.

The arrival of the A4 'Pacifics' brought a problem for the test crews for it was impossible to construct the normal indicator shelters around their smokeboxes, and Sir Nigel Gresley had instructed Tom Robson to develop a new form of steam engine indicator. The idea was to display the indicator diagrams on the screen of a cathode ray oscilloscope in the dynamometer car and record them photographically. This work kept us very busy and was all but completed when war broke out in September 1939. In the course of this work 'A4s' were not readily available and we carried out trials with an 'A1' or an 'A3' between Newcastle and Edinburgh and with a 'K3' 2-6-0 between Darlington and York, the

'Pacifics' on service trains and the 'Mogul' using the counter pressure engine. This occasion was used to get some test results for the 'K3' but the main object was to try out the indicator.

After the war the dynamometer car was used to check the working of the 'Flying Scotsman' on the new schedules, making two up and two down trips. Each of the NE, Scottish and Southern Areas claimed that its own sections involved the hardest work; in fact there was very little in it as far as average power output was concerned, slightly the highest power ouput being required in the NE Area. Tom Robson received a phone call asking for the result of the tests even before the dynamometer car had returned to Darlington: Tom, on the verge of retirement having worked well over age because of the war, bluntly replied that a third of a mile of paper record had to be examined and that the result would be stated when that had been done!

On another occasion the car was on a train to London, though not working, for tests the following day and at Peterborough the Stationmaster asked if Lord Burleigh might visit it. Chris Jarvis remembered that he was a director of the LNER and agreed, so his Lordship came in and was shown around, but as the car was not gangwayed to the train he had to stay with us all the way to London. He joined us for tea and biscuits and it was just then that a piece of coal fell off the tender of a northbound train and smashed through one of the bow windows (the car was facing north) and crashed against the closed gangway doors at the end of the car. Though not our doing, we felt that this was not quite the right sort of welcome for the former Olympic hurdles champion, but he didn't seem to mind. Charlie Trewitt imperturbably swept

up the broken glass: it was all part of the day's work.

During the 1948 interchange trials the LNER car was used on goods trains on the Western Region whilst the Swindon car was busy on the Southern. These runs involved a very early start from Old Oak Common shed and then a very late arrival back there the next evening; though arrival with a goods train was always liable to delay. The weather was exceptionally hot, well into the 90s in the non-existent shade, the brass rails inside the windows on the sunny side became too hot to touch and the drinking water ran out! On one occasion, for various reasons, the locomotive ran out of fuel and the train had to be left in sidings some miles from its destination. The engine and test car were only able to get back to base by means of some surreptitious 'borrowing' of fuel from a coal train standing in the sidings, a lump or two from each of several wagons. The temperature was still above 80 degrees Fahrenheit when we arrived back at Old Oak, at midnight.

On a further occasion when the car was out with a very heavy mineral train it was involved in so severe an impact that its roof was left with a permanent set. A very senior inspector was riding in the workshop compartment; he fell on the floor and a large heavy cupboard and its contents fell on top of him! He was rescued, not too seriously hurt, but as ill-luck would have it, a small bottle of mercury in the cupboard became uncorked and its contents found its way into the pocket containing his gold presentation watch. This was utterly ruined as gold and mercury form a pasty amalgam when they come into contact.

Life in the dynamometer car was hard work — but never dull!

Left: The board to which the intercom equipment is attached is placed on the footplate as finishing touches are put to the cable loosely clipped to the top rail of the tender. No. 706 is clearly in absolutely pristine condition, not a speck of dirt to be seen anywhere.

No. 706 was the first of the NER's three-cylinder 'Z' class 'Atlantics' (LNER class C7), which bore the brunt of important NER services until the arrival of the 'Pacifics'. Because of pressure on the Company's Workshops (Gateshead works having ceased building new locomotives in 1910) the first 20 of this class were ordered from the North British Locomotive Company, which delivered them in 1911. Later, a further 30 engines were built at Darlington.

The role of the dynamometer car in locomotive testing by E. S. COX F Inst Mech E.

IN THE first half of the present century, locomotive testing (mostly steam) involving the use of dynamometer cars, was concerned with three main objectives:

1) To confirm the ability of a locomotive to perform as its designer intended.
2) To obtain the cost in fuel and water of doing a measured amount of work in performing existing or improved schedules.
3) To provide a basis of comparison between one locomotive and another, or on the same locomotive having various modifications or alternative equipment.

To achieve any of these aims, input of energy had to be related to output. The input, in the form of coal or oil and of water, was usually quite simply measured on the locomotive itself. It was in measuring the output of energy that the dynamometer car took its place. The car's basic form could be likened to a 'spring balance on wheels' to which was added a means of recording time and speed.

This vehicle took the form of an ordinary coach, gutted of its passenger accommodation and housing, apart from facilities for the testing crew, and fitted with three principal items of equipment. First of all there was a large calibrated spring, metallic or hydraulic, capable of absorbing the greatest drawbar pull likely to be exerted by any locomotive to be tested. This spring was firmly anchored to the mainframe of the car and was connected through the normal type of coupling to the tender drawhook of the engine under test. Movement of the spring gave an indication of the drawbar pull being exerted.

Secondly there was a road wheel which could be lowered onto or withdrawn from contact with the rail by a handwheel situated inside the car. This provided for the recording of distance and speed.

The indications from these two devices were transmitted by suitable means to the third item of equipment in the car, namely the instrument table and hereon, driven from the roadwheel, was a series of rollers carrying a travelling paper chart. There was also an electric clock and instrumentation of various kinds which transferred proportional indications of drawbar pull, speed and elapsed time to electrically operated pens. The output of an integrator, which by combining pull and speed gave a measure of the work done, was also recorded.

Thus the operators in the car could observe from the moving chart all these indications at the moment of their performance. At the end of each run the test crew could obtain a summation of work done in the form of drawbar-horsepower-hours, and by withdrawing a suitable length of paper off the rolls the crew could observe a complete visual record of all aspects of the locomotive performance for inclusion in the final test report. Finally the amount of coal used to produce the output indicated by the dynamometer car readings was divided one by the other to give a figure of pounds of coal per drawbar-horsepower-hour. Although not giving a scientifically direct comparison, because it was to some extent affected by the relationship between engine weight and train weight, this figure was commercially viable, and was helpful to managers when fixing train loads and schedules and in allocating expenditure on locomotive improvement. Above all, it was useful in separating the 'sheep from the goats' when big amalgamations were afoot!

Right: Although specially posed for the photographer (as indicated by the stationary carriage outside the window) this scene depicts one of the test car crew at the recording table as he might be during a test. Percy Dobson is on the left, taking notes. The large bracket coming up through the floor was attached at its lower end to the drawgear, while its top end was attached to the recording pens. The paper roll moved from left to right, driven by the worm gear and mechanism shown on the right. The worm and gear wheel could be changed to give different paper speeds of 1ft or 2ft per mile, while for very specialised tests 22ft per mile was used — as when *Mallard* achieved its world speed record of 126mph — though for this it was necessary to change some gears in the transmission from the measuring wheel.

Facing page: A view from the back of the car, looking forward across the recording table, and its associated instruments. Clearly shown are the paper record rolls, moving in this picture from right to left. Fresh paper is on the roll on the right whilst used paper is being wound on to the roller on the lower left. Of the twin rollers above this, the right hand one was driven whilst the left hand one simply ensured paper tension during testing. The rows of pen holders were 'ticked' by electromagnets to mark various aspects of performance. Immediately above the new paper roll is the work integrator, which multiplied pull by distance and as each unit of work was recorded an electric contact ticked a pen on the paper record and moved the counter forward by one unit. The counter is the row of small discs to the right of the clock on the bench beyond the recording table. The clock was fitted with an electric contact to tick a pen on the record every two seconds. Beneath the clock four large dials are just visible which recorded distance travelled. These were later removed, but they had been adopted from the design (as the whole car was in many respects) of the GWR dynamometer car of 1904, which had come from Daniel Gooch's 'measuring wagon' of 1837, the world's first true dynamometer car. The dial immediately below the clock was probably an electric speedometer. The microphone was connected to the intercom mounted during tests on the footplate.

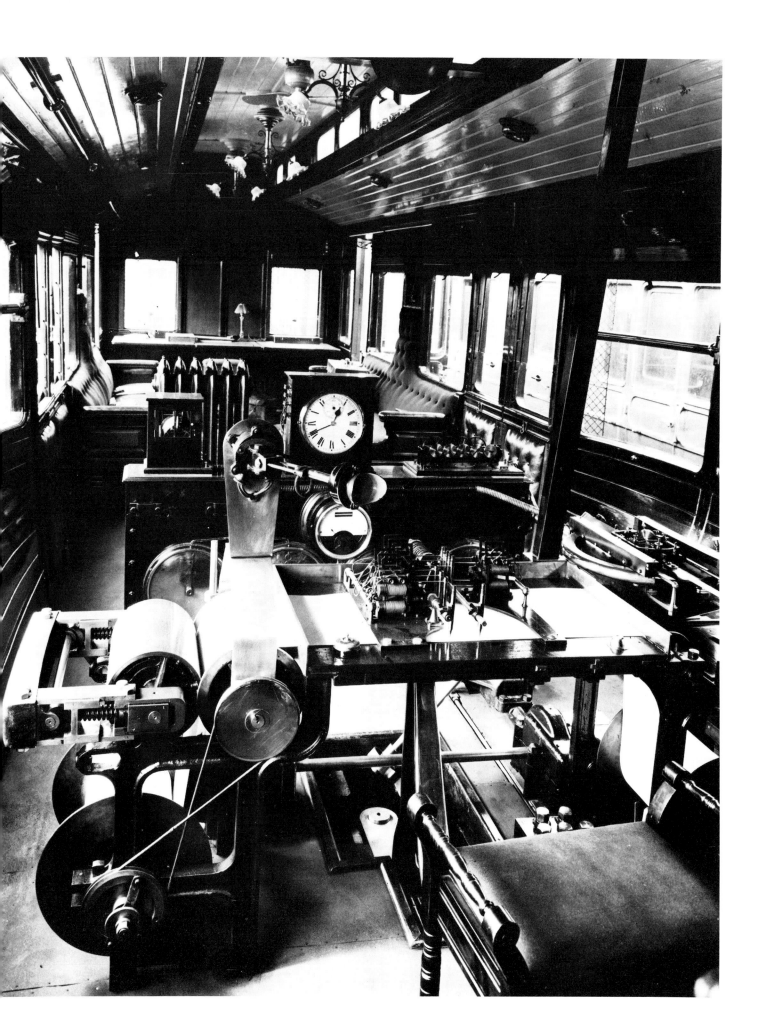

Right: Looking towards the rear of the dynamo-meter car, with the trap door in the floor open, revealing the road wheel which was lowered onto the rail to record speed and distance during locomotive tests. The inclined shaft behind the heating radiator was the drive to the mileage indicator. The electrical switch board was mounted on the back wall along with gauges for the vacuum brake and steam heating systems. The dark-suited gentleman standing in front of the door is resting his hand on one of two pillar mounted handwheels, which operated the car's handbrakes and equipment for lifting the road wheel off the rail when testing was not in progress. The long 'gauge glass' immediately to the left of this man's head measured the level of water in the locomotive's tender: this apparatus was subsequently removed and gauges placed on either side of the tender itself were observed through the 'blister' windows added to the leading end of the coach. The black trumpet-shaped object secured to the roof was the loudspeaker which relayed comments from the footplate to the test crew. The inclined wooden duct next to the recording table operator's right hand carried electric cables. Note the ornate glass lamp shades and curved panelling in the carriage sides. All the panelling and metalwork inside the car is very clean and highly polished, including the small oval works plate which reads: 'North Eastern Railway Gateshead Works 1906'.

Left: The road wheel lowered into position ready for a test to commence. This measuring wheel had a cylindrical, rather than a coned tread as on a running wheel, and if its circumference became worn by as much as 1/100th of an inch, as measured by an accurate steel tape, a new rim would be fitted to ensure accuracy of recording. This wheel was raised about 3in from the rail when not in use; more modern dynamometer cars had the measuring wheel mounted in one of the bogies rather than the main frame, as in this case. This dynamometer car, as modified for later use, is preserved as part of the National Collection at the National Railway Museum, York.

Freight

Left : Two-thirds of the LNER's revenue came from freight traffic and whilst the prestige passenger trains held most public and press attention, much work was also done by the Company to promote its fast long-distance freight services. A succession of express goods trains left King's Cross Goods Depot mid-afternoon each day, and the 'Scotch goods,' seen here getting under way on July 7 1932, was one of these. The engine in charge is 'K3' 2-6-0 No. 229, built at Darlington in 1925: note the very clean condition of the engine, even for a goods train duty. The congested state of the yard is of interest; every road is full of wagons. Limited space was used to the best advantage in this busy yard, where every turnout is on a curve.

Below right: Containerisation was not entirely new in 1928, but in that year the LNER began to extend its use for the door-to-door transport of freight. The advantage was that the consignor could load the container in his own premises, the contents then being undisturbed until they were unpacked at their destination, greatly lessening the risk of damage or pilferage during transit. The containers were made to standard designs produced by the Railway Clearing House, and illustrated here is an example of the smaller of the original two types, known as class 'A'. Initially, flat wagons were adapted to carry the containers — note the rather makeshift arrangements for securing the container to the wagon deck — but special wagons were provided later. This picture was taken on February 9 1928, following the LNER's announcement that 450 containers were to be provided, partly in view of keen competition from road transport for freight business.

Above left: In the same year the Milk Marketing Board introduced the concept of 3,000-gallon glass-lined bulk milk tankers, to replace the multitude of milk churns then in use. The dairy company provided the tank while the railway company provided the chassis. This 10ft 6in wheelbase vehicle was photographed on December 13 1928, when a number of these tankers entered traffic for carrying milk from Ingestre, Staffordshire, to the United Dairies distribution depot at Finchley. All the railway companies eventually operated these tank wagons and later, because of derailments on the Great Western Railway, a six-wheeled chassis replaced the original design. Maintenance of the tankers was the responsibility of the dairies, who washed the tanks out with hot water after every trip.

Above: Much of the LNER's freight business was generated by the heavy industry of the North East and in 1926 the contract won by Dorman Long to construct the Sydney Harbour Bridge led to a great deal of steel being fabricated into girders, all of which were transported to the docks by the LNER. In this picture NE class P3 0-6-0 (LNER class J27) No. 1028 roars past Dinsdale with a train of girders, each weighing 350-tons, en route to Middlesbrough for shipment to Australia. The photographer's original notes describe the train as weighing in excess of 1,000 tons and that it was out of gauge, thus preventing other trains passing it en route. The robust and powerful 'J27s' were the largest 0-6-0s built by the NER and No. 1028 was based at Ferryhill in 1926 as one of the oldest of its class, having been built by the North British Locomotive Company in 1908. The last J27s were completed as late as 1923, after the Grouping.

Above right: A very large electrical component weighing 38-tons manufactured by C.A. Parsons & Co. Ltd., of Newcastle upon Tyne, is inspected prior to departure. Parsons exported a great deal of electrical machinery, most of which was transported by the LNER, which built special wagons for the traffic. Known as 'trolley wagons,' these vehicles were generally classified as 'Flatrol,' which had a flat deck, and 'Weltrol,' in which the load was carried in a low-level well, between the main side members of the wagon. No. 2907 was a 'Weltrol A' built for the NER initially with a capacity of 70 tons, later uprated to 81 tons. Note the axlebox examination taking place.

Below right: Another large Parsons load, proudly carrying the name of its place of manufacture, awaits despatch on an LNER freight train. No. 6734 is a 'Weltrol D' rated at 40-tons, built before the Grouping for the NER; the LNER; built another of similar type (No. 217322) in 1938.

Previous page & right: A new bridge under construction between Doncaster and Conisborough in 1928 required the manufacture of four massive girders, each 114ft long and weighing 48 tons: all were taken to their destination by special train. The previous page shows two of the girders at York, en route to the scene of operations on June 25 1928, in the charge of an old NER class 'C' (LNER class J21) No. 534, built at Gateshead in 1890 and withdrawn in 1929. Most of this class lasted well beyond this date however, as their light axle-load made them especially useful for both passenger and freight work on branch lines. This scene contains much of interest; the signals, the wide assortment of goods wagons, the steam crane in the yard on the right and the track layout, which features at least six double slips! The extreme size of the girders — they were 9ft 7 in wide and 4ft deep — meant that they had to be secured tightly at one end, but allowed to slide at the other end on curves. The leading end was therefore fixed and the trailing end, as illustrated (right) was allowed to slide. This picture was taken while the train was parked at Haverton Hill, near Stockton.

Above: The LNER developed the trolley wagon into a massive vehicle and this 24-wheeled example, built in 1929, was capable of carrying a 150-ton load with the aid of equalising beams designed to transfer part of the weight to a pair of flanking wagons. Designated a 'Weltrol N,' the wagon is seen here at Neasden in 1931 carrying a 68ft steel girder of nearly 100 tons in weight, required for the construction of a new hotel near Marble Arch, in London. It was transferred by rail from Middlesbrough to Marylebone, and completed its journey on a 30-wheel lorry. The brake van on the right is a six-wheeled GCR vehicle coupled to assist braking.

Right: Another heavy load tackled by the LNER in 1931 aboard the 'Weltrol N' was this 63-ton stator for a 30mW alternator, built by C.A. Parsons for installation in a new power station feeding the national electricity grid. The stator is pictured after its journey from Newcastle at Mile End goods yard, where it was loaded onto a road trailer for haulage by steam tractor over the final leg of its journey.

Above: The Cunard liner *Queen Mary* was built at John Brown's yard on Clydeside and several important components were manufactured in the North East and transferred by the LNER to Middlesbrough docks for shipment to Glasgow. On Sunday September 28 1931 NER class P1 (LNER class J25) 0-6-0 No. 2058 hauled this special train of eight huge castings made by the Darlington Forge; the load was out of gauge and required complete occupation of the line. The NER practice of painting locomotive classifications on the front bufferbeam was adopted by the LNER but for many years after the Grouping the NE Area independently persisted in using the NER classifications.

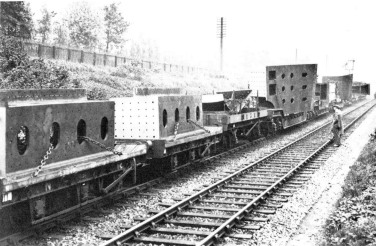

Above: Weighing in excess of 625 tons, the train made its way slowly to Middlesbrough, with utmost care taken whilst the out of gauge load passed trackside structures. The train's journey was closely watched by men on foot, as indicated in all three pictures.

Left: 'Weltrol A' No. 2907 was at work on this train of castings for the *Queen Mary* — and the reason for the complete occupation of the line is clearly apparent!

Above: A valuable export order, as well as a useful traffic for the LNER, was this train load of steam rollers, part of an order for 100 vehicles from Marshall's of Gainsborough for delivery to Greece, circa 1924. The locomotive is another J11 0-6-0, still carrying its GCR numberplates, No. 302 — renumbered 5302 by the LNER. Like all J.G. Robinson designs, the J11 was a sturdy and long-lived class, and No. 5302 was given a further lease of life by Edward Thompson in 1943, when it was one of 31 of its type rebuilt with piston valves and new cylinders.

Right: This 112-ton octagonal ingot would have been cast at the River Don Works, Sheffield, and is seen en route to Vickers Armstrong, Openshaw, Manchester, in November 1928. The vehicle carrying the ingot was known as a 'gun set,' and comprised two 60-ton capacity flat wagons, each fitted with two six-wheeled bogies, on which were mounted the girders for support of the load. The locomotive is a GCR 0-6-0 (LNER class JII). Freight of this nature was often conveyed on this line.

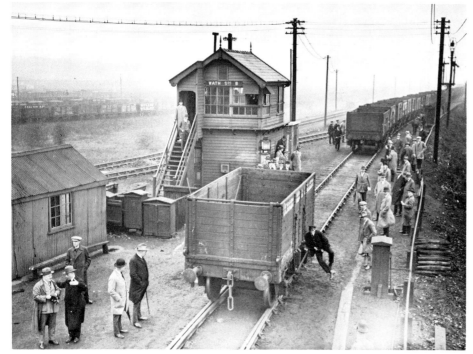

Left: Mineral traffic provided a considerable source of revenue for the LNER and there were several large marshalling yards at which loaded wagons from the pitheads were sorted into trains for despatch to delivery merchants. On May 6 1927 a party of German railway students visited Wath marshalling yard, near Barnsley. A typical large yard would have a hump over which wagons, uncoupled from each other, would be propelled, from which they would roll by gravity into the sorting sidings. It was essential to slow the wagons down as they rolled into the sidings to prevent collision damage and a brakesman would hold down a brake handle, frequently by riding on it — a distinctly hazardous operation. The empty coal wagon is marked 'Denaby Main Colliery.'

Above left: Construction of the new hump marshalling yard at March, Cambridgeshire, in 1928 was undertaken by contractors who employed their own Manning Wardle 0-6-0ST and stock, seen here on February 25 1928 moving spoil used to build the hump itself. The yard featured the mechanical retarding device for wagons developed by the Germans and installed in their own yards at Hamm, in the Ruhr. March yard was designed as the largest and most up to date facility of its type in Britain for the sorting of general goods traffic from the North for London and East Anglia, using 40 sidings capable of holding 3,679 wagons.

Left: Coal exports from Britain reached a peak in the years before the Great War of 1914-1918, as illustrated here on August 29 1907, when more than 900 wagons of coal were awaiting shipment from Grimsby Brickpit Sidings. A number of colliery names painted on the private-owner wagons remain familiar: Kiveton, Sherwood, and Sheepbridge. Of interest are the marvellous bracketed semaphore signals dotting the skyline, and the variety of sizes into which the coal has been graded, all of which would have to be carefully organised for loading into specific bunkers.

Right: The use of small, loose-coupled coal wagons of no more than 10-tons capacity, owned by the coal companies and merchants, was a very inefficient method of working, but the terminal provisions at the pits and merchants yards were geared to this wagon type and the owners had no strong desire for change. However the LNER endeavoured to encourage the use of higher capacity wagons and at the British Empire Exhibition in 1925 exhibited this 40-ton all-steel bogie hopper wagon, of which 30 were built by the Leeds Forge Company in 1923. The wagons were used in the Ashington area.

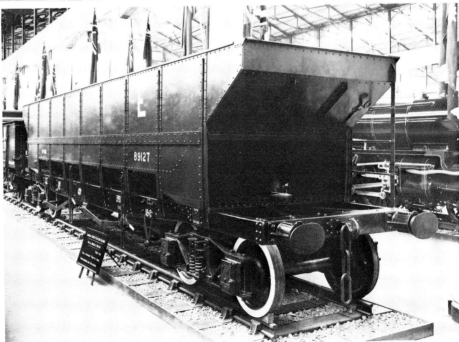

Above: The suitability of low-lying East Lincolnshire for the cultivation of potatoes resulted in an increasing amount of agricultural traffic for the LNER. One of the largest potato-growing firms in the area was W. Dennis & Sons Ltd, whose estates near Littleworth, between Peterborough and Spalding, were served by a 2ft gauge light railway, which fed an LNER private siding at Littleworth station. On 21 April 1926 petrol tractor *Billy* stands on its raised siding while its load of potatoes are transferred to the standard gauge train. The light railway covered 20 miles of track and it enabled business to continue during wet periods when the country roads of the period were waterlogged.

Right: The fireman of LNER J3 0-6-0 No. 4109 (built in 1899 at Glasgow by Dübs & Co. Ltd, which later became part of the North British Locomotive Company) watches as *Billy's* driver attends to his engine at the bottom of the ramp leading to the loading dock. The potato traffic was mainly seasonal, July and August being the busiest months of the year and at the beginning of each season six or seven special trains a day would leave the Littleworth loading dock, while the regular vegetable train (carrying potatoes to Peterborough and London principally) ran in six portions owing to the amount of the traffic. At busy periods between 200 and 400 wagons of potatoes were despatched daily from Littleworth.

Above: For many years Britain's railways relied on horse-drawn vehicles to provide road transport to and from their goods depots, but in LNER days the motor lorry began to take over this role. This small petrol-driven tractor is apparently having difficulty in manoevering a 12-ton condenser mounted on a trolley in a road which, judging by the tramlines, could be a busy one. August 22 1933.

Top & Left: This standard 30cwt Thorneycroft van was bought in some quantity by the LNER from 1927. This vehicle possessed a number of design improvements compared with other similar ones in use at the time, such as the padded seat and semi-enclosed cab for the driver, though as yet there is no windscreen, or pneumatic tyres. Little attempt was made to achieve overall harmony of design and whilst components such as mudguards and headlamps were easily replaced if damaged, they presented additional hazards in the event of a collision. CME H.N. Gresley had an overall responsibility for mechanical aspects of LNER road vehicles, but it does not appear that he took the same close personal interest in their design as he did in his locomotives and rolling stock.

Left: The first successful three-wheel road tractor was known as the Karrier 'Cob,' and had been introduced in 1930; however in 1934 the Scammell Company introduced this 25hp tow-unit with an improved coupler, and later contracts were given to this company. One of the advantages of the Scammell tractor was its very tight turning circle, demonstrated here at Farringdon Street depot, London on February 22 1934.

Right: Also taken on February 22 1934, this scene featured the Scammell at the start of a mobile test with its older rival at Farringdon Street depot. Known as 'Mechanical Horses', these tractors were produced in 3-ton and 6-ton versions and the fleet eventually ran to several hundred. The trailer was known in some areas as a 'rulley' and numerous humorous anecdotes are told about the transition from animal to mechanical traction. The older generation of horse drivers found it difficult to become accustomed to the new machines and the horse-drawn rulley was quicker, it was said, because the horse knew when to stop and start! One driver reputedly disliked getting underneath his tractor to service it — something he had never had to do with his horse!

Below right: A later model Thorneycroft lorry, but still with protruding mudguards, starting handle and springs. Photographed on December 9 1932 at King's Cross, the lorry was being loaded with part of a consignment of 5,000 cases of ingredients for making Christmas cakes and puddings despatched by Australian families for friends and relatives in this country. The consignment of gifts was described as the largest to arrive in one batch in Britain from any part of the world.

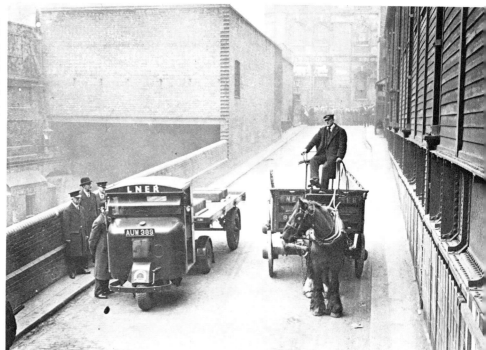

Left: The British Empire Exhibition was held at Wembley in 1924 and again in 1925 and an important feature in each year was the Palace of Engineering, in which each of the four main line Railways showed examples of their latest stock. Gresley A1 'Pacific' No. 4472 *Flying Scotsman* was a popular exhibit in both years in a highly polished finish which included the LNER coat-of-arms displayed on the cabsides. The Prince of Wales (later to become King Edward VII) performed the closing ceremony at the exhibition on November 1 1924 after which No. 4472 is seen here being removed from the Palace of Engineering — its tender already having been towed out — by GCR class L1 2-6-4T No. 342, still bearing its GCR number plate. This engine was based at Neasden until January 1925 when it moved to Gorton, and was repainted in LNER livery and renumbered 5342.

The LNER on parade

No. 4472 stands in immaculate, if rather clinical splendour, at the Exhibition in 1925: the cabside crest was retained until April 1928 when the locomotive was provided with a corridor tender in readiness for non-stop running, and the number was transferred to the cabside. In 1925 the LNER had decided to include in its display a new first class sleeping coach, which restricted space with the result that *Flying Scotsman*, normally paired with an eight-wheel tender, was coupled to a smaller six-wheeled type. The driving wheels were raised slightly off the rails and revolved slowly by means of a concealed electric motor. This photograph illustrates the perfection of finish achieved for the Exhibition: note especially the burnished buffer shanks, screw coupling, cylinder drain cocks, valve gear and sanders.

 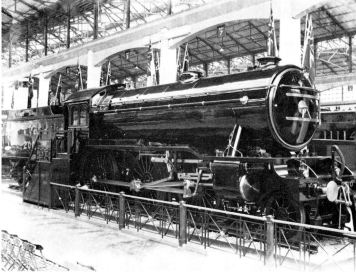

Above left: The first class sleeping carriage exhibited at Wembley in 1925 was No. 10196 (later renumbered 1235), of a new design and built the previous year at Darlington. Ten compartments were provided, each featuring washing facilities and each accommodating one passenger: an adjoining door in each compartment could be opened to create double compartments. An attendant's accommodation and toilet facilities were also included in the coach.

Above right: K3 2-6-0 No. 200, at that time a new mixed traffic engine, was also featured on the 1925 display stand. No. 200, built earlier that year at Darlington as the last of a batch of 50 engines, was painted in black livery, lined in red. The first Gresley design to be built by the former NER workshops, the 'K3s' were originally introduced on the GN in 1920, and 193 were built altogether: the last example emerged from Darlington in 1937. This class had a massive 6ft diameter boiler and was very successful in a wide range of duties including all types of freight, express passenger and excursion working.

The Prince of Wales visited Doncaster works in October 1926 and amongst the rolling stock lined up for his inspection were 'Pacific' No. 2553 *Manna*, the Stirling 'Single' No. 1 and class P1 2-8-2 No. 2394, seen here in the works yard. The 'Pacific', built at Doncaster in 1924, had recently been overhauled prior to returning to King's Cross (its home shed) for express work on the GN main line. Named originally after the racehorse which won the Derby and the '2,000 Guineas' in 1925, No. 2553 was renamed *Prince of Wales* in November 1926 in honour of the Royal visit, the name *Manna* later being given to 'Pacific' No. 2596, built in 1930. No. 2394 was one of two 2-8-2s, basically heavy freight versions of Gresley's 'Pacifics', which were at first fitted with booster engines on the trailing wheels to give additional power when starting, or when climbing steep gradients. The pair spent their lives working mineral trains between New England Yard, Peterborough and the GN coal railhead at Ferme Park, Hornsey, were the coal was bagged and distributed by the merchants.

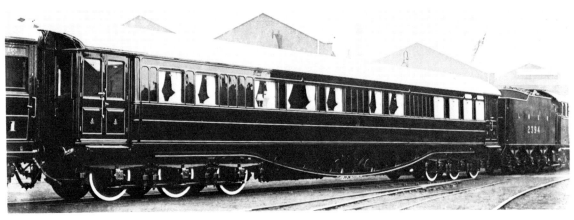

Left: also inspected at Doncaster by the Prince of Wales was the Queen's Saloon, part of the LNER's Royal Train. The two royal saloons had just been refurbished at Doncaster, the varnished teak exterior panelling having been given special attention. The coach was No. 395, but apart from the royal coat-of-arms on the doors, no other lettering, insignia or numbers appeared on the panelling.

Right: This amazing scene at Southend station on July 2 1933 was a popular feature of local exhibitions and displays, which the LNER made a great feature of, especially in the 1930s. These exhibitions were part of the Company's general public relations work with the money collected being donated to charity. The display of engines and stock was supplemented by rides like this, where 72 people were hoisted in the air in the body of a 10-ton wagon, and then rotated in a full circle. Adults were charged 2d and children 1d. 'Don't miss this novelty' proclaims the blackboard on the wagon side. Note that the crane is anchored to the rails, for stability. Also for 1d a time, visitors could pull off a signal, or ride in a platelayers 'velocipede.'

Below: The Southend display in July 1933 featured No. 4472 *Flying Scotsman*, as well as No. 10000 and, in stark contrast, an old GER class Y5 0-4-0T No. 7230, which was built at Stratford in 1903 and was normally used on shunting duties at Stratford Carriage Works. More than 21,000 people visited this exhibition.

Right: Another attraction offered at the LNER exhibitions was a ride in a trailer towed by a Lister auto-truck (for a 1d fare), as in this scene at Romford, on June 6 1936. The attendance at this event was 26,000 and £800 was raised for charity. The exhibits included 'Pacific' No. 2750 *Papyrus*, which the previous year had achieved a speed of 108mph whilst descending Stoke Bank on a special run from Newcastle to London, in preparation for the introduction of the 'Silver Jubilee' service. Other locomotives on show and pictured here included the renowned GER 4-4-0 No. 8900 *Claud Hamilton*, recently rebuilt in the Gresley style, and class B12 4-6-0 No. 8579, also rebuilt with a larger boiler and round-topped firebox. Nevertheless both engines displayed the traditional GER polished steel ring on the smokebox door.

Above: The Romford exhibition was also the occasion for the official naming of class B17 No. 2858 *The Essex Regiment*, seen here being prepared for the grand unveiling of its name-plates. The van in the distance to the right of the engine advertises the LNER's 'high-class 10-hour furniture removal service', while in the left distance a locomotive boiler is just visible.

Right:No. 2858 is officially named on June 6 1936 by Lt.Col A.E. Maitland DSO MC, Commanding Officer of the 1st Battalion, the Essex Regiment, while a squad of his men provide a guard of honour, complete with rifles and fixed bayonets. No. 2858 had previously run trials as *Newcastle United*, one of the 'Footballer' series of B17s, turned out from Darlington only a few weeks before. A touring camping coach and a Pullman are included in the display in front of the B17.

Left: On June 22 1935 B17 No. 2845 was named *The Suffolk Regiment* at Ipswich by Sir John Ponsonby, the Colonel of the Regiment. LNER representatives at the ceremony included Chairman William Whitelaw, Chief General Manager Sir Ralph Wedgwood and Chief Mechanical Engineer H. N. Gresley. Although most of the B17 4-6-0s were built at Darlington, none were permanently stationed in the NE area. Proposals for a batch to be built for service there were made on two occasions, but each time the Area management successfully expressed a preference for more mixed traffic engines.

Below: This marvellous scene at King's Cross took place on June 20 1939, just a few weeks before the Second World War broke out on September 3 1939. Class V2 2-6-2 No. 4844, brand new from Doncaster, was named *Coldstreamer* in the presence of the band of the Coldstream Guards and LNER Chairman Sir Ronald Matthews, pictured here making his speech. For the next 12 years *Coldstreamer* worked from King's Cross shed, in which time it assisted with the tremendous amount of wartime traffic on the East Coast Main Line. In 1951 the engine was sent to St Margaret's shed, Edinburgh, where it remained until withdrawal at the end of 1962.

One of the locomotives featured at an LNER exhibition at New Barnet in June 1937 was 'A4' No. 4482 *Golden Eagle*, here receiving the rapt attention of a small boy, smartly attired in striped school blazer, short trousers and with neatly brushed hair! *Golden Eagle* was the first of 31 'A4s' built at Doncaster in the years 1936-38. Stationed initially at King's Cross for two years, then transferred to Haymarket shed for the next three years, the engine spent most of its life working from Gateshead shed.

Below: The 'PR' value of the huge and impressive 2-8-0 + 0-8-2 Beyer Garratt locomotive No. 2395 was not overlooked by the publicity-conscious LNER. The massive locomotive is seen here on April 1 1930 at Sheffield Victoria station, at an exhibition of special freight rolling stock to which 400 traders were invited as guests of the LNER and Sheffield Rotary Club. No. 2395, pictured carrying the insignia of Rotary International, was normally only used for banking heavy coal trains on the Worsborough bank, near Wath. Coupled to the Garratt is the largest wagon set built in Britain at that time: the 1929-built 'Weltrol N' complete with the enormous cantilevers which spread the load to two neighbouring wagons, which enabled the assembly to carry a maximum weight of 150 tons, with a total overall weight of 370 tons.

The Stockton & Darlington Railway Centenary, 1925

The Stockton & Darlington Railway had been opened on September 27 1825 and its Centenary was celebrated at the beginning of July 1925, a few months early, to coincide with the tenth session of the International Railway Conference. The LNER masterminded the Centenary celebrations, the main features being an exhibition of locomotives, stock, permanent way and signalling equipment at Faverdale Works, Darlington, and a procession of locomotives and trains, including a tableau train depicting the part played by the wheel in the evolution of civilisation. Incidentally, the LNER also chose the S&D Anniversary of September 27 in 1935 to run the trial trip of its new 'Silver Jubilee' express from King's Cross, with pioneer 'A4 Pacific' No. 2509 *Silver Link*

Left: The memorial tablet designed by Stephen Wilkinson FRIBA, unveiled at Stockton station by HRH the Duke of York, later to become King George VI. The coat-of-arms of the LNER with its proud motto 'Forward' is prominent at the top of the tablet. The massive impact of railways on mankind is clearly reflected in the wording of the tablet.

Above: The locomotives taking part in the Centenary procession were marshalled in the exhibition grounds, each carrying a number on the top lamp bracket, in the order in which they were due to run. First was the Hetton Colliery 0-4-0 locomotive built by George Stephenson in 1822 at the Hetton Colliery workshops. It was rebuilt in 1857 and again in 1882, when the link motion was fitted. Second was the *Derwent* of 1845, designed by Timothy Hackworth and built by Kitchings of Hopetown Foundry, Darlington, for service on the S&DR. By the time exhibit No. 3 was built, locomotives had come to assume their well-known style of appearance, this 0-6-0 having been built in 1867 to the design of William Wheatley for the North British Railway.

Left: The Hetton Colliery locomotive was George Stephenson's first successful attempt at building a steam engine. It is now part of the National Collection and can be seen at the North of England Open Air Museum, Beamish, Co. Durham.

Right: It is doubtful that the Hetton Colliery locomotive's drivers were all quite as smartly turned out as this footplateman at the Centenary celebrations. The driving position was certainly very exposed while the fireman worked from what later developed into the footplate and cab; a boiler gauge glass on the backhead is visible in this view.

Below: 0-6-0 *Derwent* was listed as No. 25 in the S&DR lists: note the primitive spectacle plate, probably a later addition. Also part of the National Collection, this engine is preserved at the North Road Museum, Darlington.

Bottom: No. 4 in the Centenary procession had been an 1874-built S&DR 0-6-0, followed by a series of later locomotives designed for mineral or fast goods working, including three Gresley designs: 'K3' 2-6-0 No. 203, 'O2' 2-8-0 No. 3499 and the first 'P1' 2-8-2 No. 2393, only just completed at Doncaster. Passenger locomotives commenced with this locomotive, a full-sized replica of the GWR broad gauge 2-2-2 *North Star*, the original having been built in 1837. Towed on a 'Weltrol', without its chimney (to conform with loading gauge restrictions) the locomotive lacked some of its normal dignity and impact! The towing engine is J71 0-6-0T No. 181, built at Darlington in 1890; the wagon is a GW vehicle, known on its home territory as a 'Crocodile.'

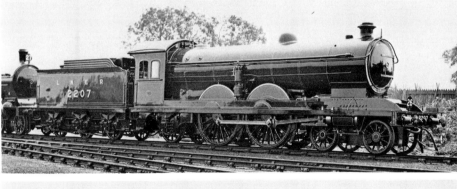

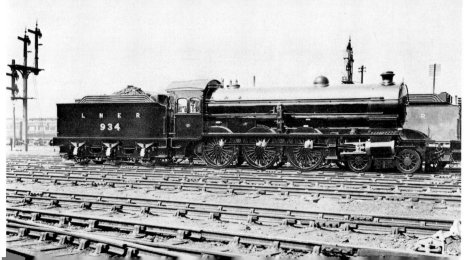

Above: Three other famous 'Singles' were featured, including this Midland Railway 'Spinner,' No. 679, built at Derby in 1899. The other engines were Patrick Stirling's GNR 4-2-2 No. 1 with 8ft driving wheels, built in 1870, and GCR 4-2-2 No. 5972, designed by Harry Pollitt and built in 1900. What a superb line-up of road vehicles lines the track beyond the engine!

Left, below: The first modern engine in the procession was NER mixed traffic 4-6-0 (LNER class B16) No. 934, built in 1921 at Darlington to the design of Sir Vincent Raven. This class ultimately numbered 70, including 32 examples built in 1923 after the Grouping. The 'B16s' were powerful locomotives with three cylinders and a tractive effort of 30,311lb. Sir Nigel Gresley and Edward Thompson rebuilt some 'B16s' in accordance with their own principles, both variations being fitted with outside Walschaerts valvegear.

Left, above: Exhibit No. 26 in the display was No. 2207, one of the NE 'Z' class 'Atlantics,' its Saxony green livery having been replaced by the slightly lighter GNR apple green which the LNER adopted for its most powerful passenger engines. The locomotive just visible on the left is NER 'S' class No. 2006, one of the first 4-6-0s to be used in Britain for passenger work. It was awarded a Gold Medal at the Paris Exhibition of 1900

Right: Gresley's magnificent 2-8-0 + 0-8-2 'Garratt' No. 2395, newly completed by Beyer Peacock at Manchester and not yet introduced into traffic, impresses the spectators in the Centenary procession. The locomotive consisted basically of two three-cylinder engines of the 'O4' class used for mineral workings on the GN main line, supplied with steam by a massive single boiler, 7ft in diameter, and with a total heating surface of 3,510 sq ft and a grate area of 56.3 sq.ft. The engine had a tractive effort of 72,940lbs at 85% of boiler pressure, and the boiler had 259 tubes, 45 superheater flues and a working pressure of 180psi. It was the most powerful locomotive to be built in Britain at the time. After electrification of the Manchester-Sheffield & Wath line the Garratt was transferred to banking duties on the Lickey incline, from Bromsgrove, and converted to oil firing. It was withdrawn from service in 1955.

The NER had operated a number of petrol-driven railcars and this example, No. 2105 had been built in 1923 to carry 40 passengers. It was unusual in that it possessed a bogie at one end and a single pair of wheels at the other. The engine was placed above the bogie, the drive being taken to the single axle. The vehicle was slightly more than 38ft long with a tare weight of 17tons 5cwt. Note the dumb buffers and lack of conventional drawgear, emergency couplings only being provided. The car was powered by a a six-cylinder Daimler sleeve-valve engine capable of developing 100hp at 1,200rpm, this giving the car a top speed of 40mph on the level and 30mph on most gradients. Petrol was fed to the engine by gravity from two tanks, and two radiators (one at each end) were fitted. Power was transmitted through a three-speed gearbox and a multiple disc fibre-and-steel clutch: drive was thence through a propeller shaft, two universal joints and hollow torque tube to the single axle. The railcar was fitted with the Westinghouse brake and compressed air was provided from a small pump fitted in tandem with the engine.

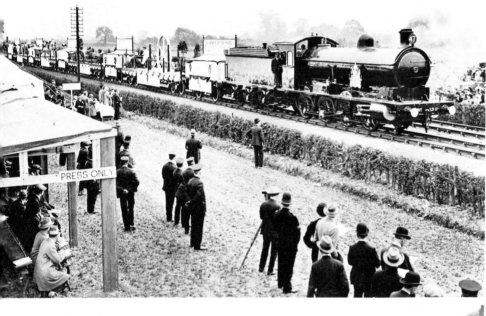

Above: One of the heaviest NER 0-8-0 freight engines, class T3 (LNER class Q7) No. 904 passes with a train of mixed mineral wagons consisting of 10½-ton chaldron vehicles followed by larger capacity 20-ton and 40-ton wagons. All are of the hopper, or self-discharging type. The Q7 was the last of the series of four classes of NER 0-8-0s, each an improvement on its predecessor. Raven fitted the locomotive with three cylinders, each having its own set of Stephenson valve gear, located between the frames.

Left, above: The Centenary Procession tableau train was hauled by an older 0-8-0, No. 130, one of the first of the type, built for the NER in 1902. The tableau was in six parts, the first being allegorical, the second representing the first wheel, cut by prehistoric men from the forest, and the third depicting the progress of the wheel from the Pharoahs to the stage-coach. Tableau IV was devoted to the theme of beauty whilst the fifth introduced the most famous chapter — the history of the wheel from Stephensons's experiments with engine building, and finally tableau VI suggested the world-wide use of railways.

Left, below: In tableau V, the figure of George Stephenson is surrounded by a group of friends and colliery blacksmiths, together with a replica of the tiny smithy at Hetton Colliery, with its forge bellows and anvils. A model of *Locomotion* is also visible behind the top-hatted men.

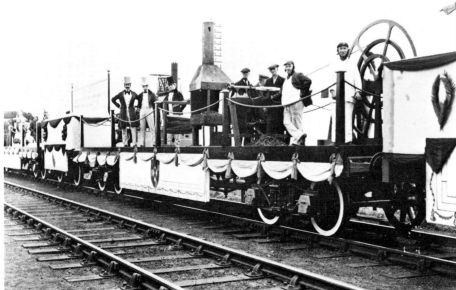

Above: Last in the procession was a train of chaldron wagons of the 1825 period, together with a coach described as 'the long coach of the S&DR Company'. This was a replica of the original train which ran at the opening of the S&DR a century before when the Company Directors rode in the coach whilst lesser mortals filled the wagons. *Locomotion No. 1* was employed to haul the train, powered by a petrol engine in its tender whilst oily rags were burned to provide smoke. The signals are showing a clear road ahead for the train as it rolls rather majestically into Stockton station, with the Darlington Band in the last wagon.

Right above: The electric locomotives were well away from any source of current and thus had to be towed around by steam engines. No. 13 was the prototype express locomotive intended for use on the NER line between York and Newcastle, a project once high in priority but which never came to fruition in LNER days. The locomotive was repainted in LNER livery for the procession but it otherwise languished at Darlington until it was eventually sold for scrap in 1950. It had undergone trials on the Newport-Shildon line.

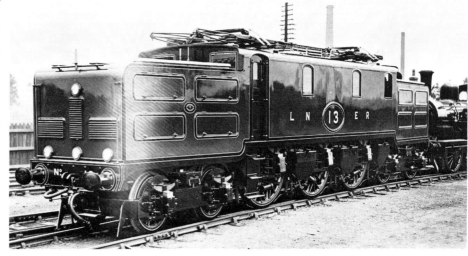

Right, below: No. 9 was one of ten Bo-Bo locomotives employed on the line between Shildon and Newport, which had been electrified in 1915 but which reverted to steam operation in 1935, by which time its coal traffic had fallen to 15% of that carried when the electrification had been planned. Tentative proposals were made in 1927 to convert one of these locomotives to diesel-electric operation, but nothing came of this project.

Above left: After the procession, many of the locomotives were exhibited in sidings adjoining those locomotives and stock already on display. *Locomotion* is seen here at rest after hauling the replica train. This locomotive is also now part of the National Collection and together with *Derwent* may today be seen at the North Road Museum, Darlington.

Above right: 0-4-0 *Invicta* was another early locomotive present for the celebrations: it was built by Robert Stephenson in 1830 (the year the Liverpool & Manchester Railway opened) for the Canterbury & Whitstable Railway, in Kent. The cylinder dimensions — 10in diameter by 18in stroke, are painted on the cylinder cladding. The wheels were 4ft in diameter and the boiler pressure was just 40psi. *Invicta* is now restored and displayed in Canterbury.

Rolling stock from the London Underground system was also included in the Centenary celebrations. These included (left) an early electric locomotive from the City & South London Railway, dating from its opening in 1890, together with a C&SL bogie vehicle (centre) and a new carriage for the Highgate tube service (right).

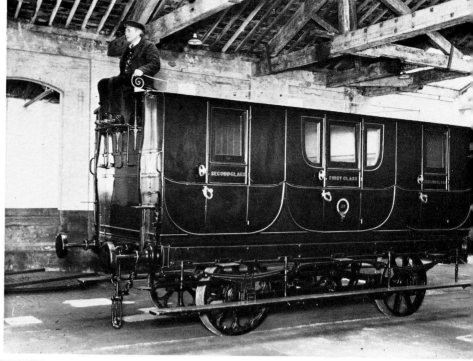

Right: This 1850 four-wheeled composite coach, with a single first class compartment flanked by a second class compartment on each side, is a fine example of coachbuilding craftsmanship. The relatively low roof allowed for a certain amount of luggage to be carried 'on top' with the guard, who was in a remarkably exposed position. The vehicle's stagecoach ancestry is clear.

Below: First class passengers enjoyed the luxury of leather upholstery, but third class ticket holders, although no longer travelling in wooden wagons, were seated back-to-back in these spartan conditions on solid benches, the only daylight coming from windows in the doors.

Above: This early luggage van also had basic accommodation for a guard. Note the brake wheel, alarm bell and top light.

Left: The sloping-sided chaldron type of wagon was still widely used in the NE more than a century after this early example was built for the S&DR. Note the sturdy construction, lifting end door and the hefty brake blocks acting on both wheels.

Just after midnight on Saturday February 29 1908, a rear-end collision occurred on the GCR between Woodhouse East and West Junctions, near Sheffield, involving these two 4-4-0s. The engines were double-heading a special train conveying emigrants en-route to Liverpool for embarkation to the United States of America when they ran into the back of a mineral train at about 20mph. The fireman of the leading engine and the goods guard both lost their lives but although the first coach was telescoped only one of the 200 passengers was slightly injured. The cause of the collision is uncertain, the evidence being insufficient to decide whether there had been a signalling error or if the passenger train had passed signals at danger.

The two 4-4-0s were from a class built for the Manchester Sheffield & Lincolnshire Railway between 1887 and 1894, known on the GCR as class 2. The LNER reclassified the engines as 'D7s' and No. 711 (below) was built by Kitson & Co Ltd of Leeds, and lasted until 1933.

Mishaps

THE UP 'Norfolk Coast Express', the 1pm departure from Cromer to Liverpool Street, was in collision with a light engine at Colchester on July 12 1913, when the crew of 4-6-0 No. 1506 and the train guard were killed. Despite the destruction of several coaches there were no fatalities on the train. The incident was caused by a signalman's error: he had forgotten about the light engine, the driver of which became alarmed when he saw the signals off for the express and sent his fireman to the signalbox. Seeing the express bearing down on him, he started his engine to minimise the impact, which would otherwise have been much more severe. The collision caused considerable public criticism.

Right: This view of No. 1506 after the crash shows the extent of the damage sustained by the 4-6-0. Its bogie has been torn off — a set of wheels are lying alongside the tender — and the engine was withdrawn and scrapped. Although the locomotive was replaced in a later batch of new engines, the actual number remained vacant, even when the 'B12s' were renumbered by the LNER in 1946.

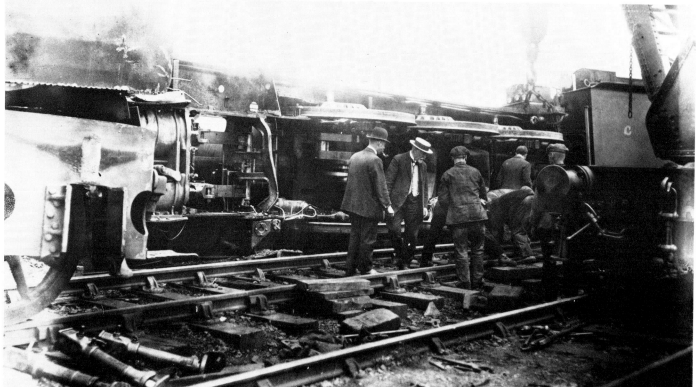

Above: The 4-6-0's cylinders, slide bars, distorted motion bracket and crank axle are visible in this picture of the aftermath of this major mishap, as a steam crane gets to grips with clearance operations.

Right: The stricken 'B12' is still lying on its side, although dismantling has apparently started: the chimney certainly seems to have disappeared together with much of the mangled wreckage around the smokebox, presumably in readiness for lifting the engine hulk. The light engine involved in the incident, 2-4-0 No. 471, is visible on the right. This engine escaped relatively unscathed, though its tender was damaged beyond repair and scrapped.

Above left: The force of No. 1506's impact with the 2-4-0 is readily apparent from this view of the front of No. 471's tender: the heavy plate main frames have been bent into a tight 'S' immediately behind the second axle and the leading spring has been torn off.

Above right: Passengers from the ill-fated express view the terrible wreckage of the train's leading carriages, which were completely destroyed as a result of extensive telescoping.

Left: A train of empty coaching stock was being shunted in sidings at Finsbury Park on November 21 1923 when the last coach was forced over the buffer stop, demolishing part of the retaining wall which collapsed into Stroud Green Road. Nobody was injured and the coach stopped short of falling into the street below: the vehicle is seen straddling the concrete stopblock at the end of the siding. Carriage No. 8431 (GNR numbering) was a brake second, originally built as one half of an articulated pair, and altered in 1921 to form part of a quadruple articulated set.

ON SATURDAY June 15 1935 the 10.45pm express from King's Cross to Newcastle was run in two parts, the second part leaving at 10.53pm hauled by Ivatt 'Atlantic' No. 4441. The 11-coach train was checked to about 20mph by signals at Welwyn Garden City, where it was run into from the rear at nearly 70mph by the following newspaper train to Leeds, hauled by 'K3' 2-6-0 No. 4009. The rear coach of the Newcastle express was utterly destroyed by the enormous impact and every person travelling in it died. The coach frame, as shown above, was twisted virtually beyond recognition. Nevertheless, the collision demonstrated the value of the buckeye couplings which were a standard fitting on LNER corridor stock, for apart from the last vehicle, all those with buckeye couplers remained upright and in line until they came to rest. Thirteen passengers were killed and 81 injured. The collision was attributed to a signalman's error, but a weakness was also found in the track circuiting arrangements, as a result of which a revised system was adopted by the LNER and this became known as 'Welwyn Control'.

Right: Amidst a litter of bogies and debris steam cranes clear wrecked carriages at Welwyn Garden City on June 16 1935, after the major mishap of the previous day.

Vintage motive power

Left, above: This 1870s scene at Doncaster works depicts the work of two eminent GNR locomotive engineers of the Victorian era. No. 513 (left) is a Stirling 0-4-4 well tank, of 1874, employed for more than 30 years on London suburban duties, whilst No. 276 was built in 1866 by the Avonside Engine Co., almost at the end of Archibald Sturrock's period in office. This engine also served on Metropolitan duties in London, on which the class was superseded by Stirling's 0-4-4Ts.

Left, below: Stirling 8ft 'Single' No. 221 stands at the main arrival platform at King's Cross in the 1880s: the locomotive was built at Doncaster in 1876 and is in immaculate condition. It has been uncoupled from the train and is ready to run forward to clear the crossover and then run back along No. 2 platform to reach the station locomotive shed for preparation in readiness for its run back to Grantham, where it was stationed at the time. Later in its career No. 221 lost its domeless boiler and brass safety valve bonnet when it was given an Ivatt domed-boiler, and cab with extended roof in 1899. The engine was re-fitted with a domeless boiler in 1907 and withdrawn in 1909.

Below: In contrast to the comfortable bogie coaches of the 1930s, the 'Flying Scotsman' of the 1890s was made up of short-wheelbase carriages distinguished by the flat roofs and continuous footboards of the East Coast Joint Stock of the era, designed by Great Northern Carriage & Wagon Superintendent E. F. Howlden. The locomotive is one of the NER 'M' class 4-4-0s, which distinguished themselves in the 'race to Aberdeen' in the summer of 1895. Although restaurant cars were beginning to be introduced on the East Coast services, the 'Flying Scotsman', seen here passing Dunbar, was not one of the first trains to be provided with catering services and it continued to stop at York for 20 minutes to enable passengers to take a hurried, late lunch. This was of course North British territory, but NER engines worked to and from Edinburgh, a practice preceding the Grouping by many years.

Above: The GNR Stirling 'Single' No. 1 was used in the S&DR Centenary celebrations of 1925, after which it appeared at several local exhibitions, and it is pictured here in March 1927 at the original York station (since abandoned) prior to entering the neighbouring LNER Railway Museum. The elegant 4-2-2 provides a diminutive contrast to 'A1' 4-6-2 No. 2579 *Dick Turpin*, built by the North British Locomotive Company, and shedded at Heaton.

Right: The LNER made the most of the 'Flying Scotsman' service's 50th anniversary in 1938. Not only were more 'A4's' built and the two trains provided with entirely new coaches, but No. 1 was returned to steam for excursion work. Here we see the 'Single' on June 30 1938, with a special from King's Cross at Stevenage, where its passengers transferred to the new 'Flying Scotsman' train hauled by No. 4498 *Sir Nigel Gresley*. No. 1's stock comprised late 19th century flat-roofed teak panelled stock still in service. Stevenage station in 1938 was a conventional GNR structure in a rural setting, very different to the station of today, with its industrial surroundings. Wearing a cloth cap in the group of four men alongside the lamp post is Inspector Sam Jenkins.

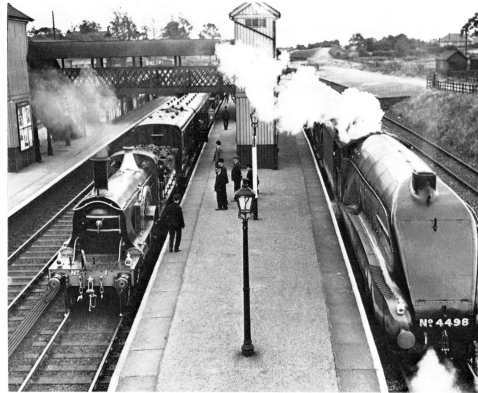

Above: The two special trains of June 30 1938 leave Stevenage simultaneously, *Sir Nigel Gresley* giving way on the fast line to No. 1, which appeared in GNR livery similar to that adopted by the LNER, except that the GNR colours featured a darker shade of green on the outer edges of the tender sides. The GNR 'somersault' semaphores have been replaced by LNER upper quadrants.

Left: Apart from the upper quadrant signals just visible beyond the bridge, this 1938 picture presents a convincing reconstruction of the East-Coast Main Line scene of 50 years previously. After the Stevenage photo-session No. 4498 turned on to the down fast line, running to Barkston, near Grantham, where the train reversed on the triangular junction before returning to London. No. 1 and its train of vintage stock ran on the slow line to Hitchin where the engine turned prior to running back to the capital.

Built at Doncaster in 1870, No. 1 was withdrawn from service in September 1907, having run 1,404,663 miles. It was stored until 1908 when it was restored for display at the Imperial International Exhibition, London, along with Ivatt 'Atlantic' No. 1442. No. 1 was then kept at the King's Cross shed erecting shop until November 1924 when it was restored at Doncaster for the Centenary Celebrations.

Right: Nearly three years after the LNER had vanished into the national system, a special run took place on November 26 1950 to commemorate the withdrawal of the last of the renowned Ivatt 'Atlantics', which had been an everyday part of life on the GN main line for almost 50 years. The large 'Atlantics' were withdrawn over a period of seven years, the first to disappear being LNER No. 4459 in 1943. The last engine in service was LNER No. 3294, seen here as BR No. 62822 (built at Doncaster in 1905) heading the 'Ivatt Atlantic Special' away from King's Cross. The special left the terminus at 11am on a rather foggy morning, but this did nothing to dampen the spirits of the many railwaymen and enthusiasts who gathered at the stations and tracksides to bid farewell to the last of this popular class of locomotives.

The works plate from the leading right-hand wheel-splasher was mounted on a polished wooden plaque and is seen (above left) being presented at Doncaster by C. K. Bird, Chief Regional Officer of BR Eastern Region, to H. G. Ivatt, the son of H. A. Ivatt who had introduced the engines during his period as Locomotive Superintendent of the Great Northern Railway (1896-1911). The 'Atlantic' was later placed on public display, when its controls were explained to interested visitors to the footplate, (above right).

GCR Staff at Marylebone, 1907

Above left: In this period, the Railways of Britain were the country's biggest carrier of people and freight, and engine drivers were regarded as a social elite: this driver is clearly well aware of the fact, and proud of his responsible position. He is seemingly happy to be photographed with his scrupulously clean oilcan in hand: the gold watch chain indicates another 'tool of the trade' — punctuality was doubtless fastidiously maintained. Although he has not been provided with a distinctive uniform he nevertheless gives his overalls and cloth cap the dignity his important job deserves.

Above right: In contrast, this young fireman seems a little self-conscious at being photographed: he is clutching a wad of cheesecloth which would be used both for polishing cab fittings and also for protecting his hands whilst working the hot handles of the injector steam valves, blower and firehole door. His engine is GCR class 9L 4-4-2T No. 1127, one of a batch of 12 engines delivered by Beyer Peacock in 1907 and allocated to Neasden for working the Marylebone suburban services. These locomotives were transferred to other duties after the introduction of the larger 4-6-2Ts, in 1911. This fireman's tour of duty would probably have included a couple of round trips to High Wycombe or Aylesbury.

Left: This passenger guard, posed as if waiting to give the rightaway, is wearing a splendid uniform which is almost Prussian in style with its double-breasted tunic, brass buttons and trousers complete with red stripe down the sides. Chains for his watch and whistle are part of the outfit whilst his boots and chinstrap are well polished. There is no doubt about his status, emphatically stated on his collar.

Right: Those who believe that a lack of respect for authority dates from the time when policemen were permitted to wear a collar and tie will gain support from this view of GCR constable No. 61! An undisputed guardian of law and order, he too sports a luxuriant moustache of the type to become famous in the war years when Kitchener's likeness was featured on thousands of posters proclaiming 'Your country needs you!'

Below: The ticket collector's uniform is rather less intimidating than that of the guard; it is possibly of older pattern. The jacket and waistcoat are cutaway, compared with the higher collar of the guard, to reveal a high stiff collar and tie. His ticket clippers are ready for work and his serious countenance will doubtless discourage any attempts to pass the barrier without the correct piece of pasteboard!

Right: Left luggage offices were much the same in 1907 as they are today: the interior unseen by most travellers, but performing a necessary service nonetheless. Once again, the office attendant's uniform is worn with pride: his cap and collar carry the GCR initials and the watch chain is once again in evidence.

Left: This Foreman Porter's uniform does not display his grade, merely the elaborate GCR initials on his collar and cap. The heavy serge cloth of the uniform did not lend itself easily to pressing trousers into sharp creases, but the high collar and tie are immaculately presented.

Below left: This profile of a Marylebone passenger porter looks almost as if he is modelling a new military style of uniform, very similar to that worn by the passenger guard on page 99. The GCR initials on his epaulettes are in bold serified capitals in contrast to the more intricate — and possibly more difficult to read — style shown on the Foreman Porter's jacket. The advertisement for the magazine 'Motor Traction' states that it deals with 'motor vehicles for business purposes' and that it is published every Saturday, price 1d!

Below right: The same porter stands on the platform weighing scales at Marylebone, adjacent to a large cabinet full of destination labels which had to be pasted onto passengers' luggage.

Above left: The shunter's job, involving the coupling or uncoupling of wagons with a pole and applying the handbrake on moving wagons to slow them down or bring them to rest could be hazardous. Note the differing wagons ends: the Stephenson Clarke 10-tonner has a top-hinged end, whilst the other has a solid end with strong angle irons strengthening the seven-plank construction.

Above right: This goods guard is wearing yet another variety of GCR uniform. As might be expected, the watch chain features prominently in the waistcoat, which appears to have leather sleeves, these being hard wearing enough to stand up to a good deal of manual work. The polka-dot scarf adds a touch of colour and individuality and indicates that this man's job would have been cold and uncomfortable, at the tail-end of a loose coupled goods train. He would need to be constantly alert, to aid the driver in slowing and stopping the train, and to watch for hot axleboxes and other likely causes of out-of-course delays.

Left: A goods porter worked hard for low wages, but this chap seems quite happy at his work, apparently on a warm day in 1907. Note the long-sleeved woollen undervest and rolled up shirt sleeves and the uniform waistcoat, with lapels. The stout wooden case is marked 'Huntley & Palmers Biscuits.' Whose was the bowler hat on the wall — the photographer's? Nothing was wasted on the GCR: the kerb behind the porter is an old rail.

Facing page: This is a superb photograph containing much atmosphere and a good deal of interesting detail. You can almost smell the horse and hear its hooves clopping on the road! The carter had a cold job in poor weather, perched on his open seat, high above the road. He would need the leather apron, jacket and top coat he is wearing here to repel the cold and rain. Note the detail of the cart, the bag of oats hung on its frame and the shiny horse brasses.

Above right: The wheeltapper's job was monotonous but important: how often, one wonders, did he discover a cracked wheel or a loose tyre? The sound has disappeared from today's railway but the rhythmic 'ting' of his long-handled hammer will be a vivid memory for many people. The wheeltapper is not kitted out in any sort of formal uniform, but his pin-striped trousers are accompanied by an official issue denim jacket carrying the inscription 'C&W Dept' on the collar.

Above: The GCR evidently took train cleanliness seriously and this carriage cleaner is busy sweeping out a first class vehicle, judging by the button-down leather upholstery and the lace antimacassars. The GCR coach livery of the period was brown and cream, later changed to a teak finish. Closer inspection of this cleaner reveals that it's about time he applied for a new waistcoat!

Right: This permanent way lengthman and his lookout are taking their role very seriously indeed for the photographer's benefit. Their clothing is practical, enabling them to carry out their work without hindrance, yet keeping out the worst of the weather. This was many years before it was decided that men working on the track should be readily visible by wearing bright clothing, rather than wear an effective form of camouflage.

Left: At the 'country' end of Marylebone's platform 4, two women porters deputising for men during the Great War in 1915 are loading a barrow with wicker baskets. These two energetic ladies make no concession to female fashion, even to the cloth caps into which hair is tucked, or tied into a 'bun'. By 1916 the GCR employed 1,526 women who worked as ticket collectors, porters and cleaners.

Carriage cleaning was hard and tedious work, but the GCR evidently tried to maintain its standards of presentation even during the strained days of the war. This 1915 view shows one of the Company's women cleaners tackling a teak-finish panelled coach at Marylebone station. Panelled stock was particularly difficult to clean, with grime and dirt accumulating in the rounded corners. This view illustrates the craftsmanship put into carriage building of the era.

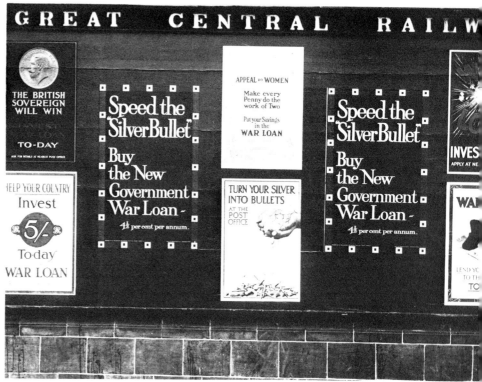

Right, Below: These symmetrically arranged poster displays at Marylebone, photographed in August 1915, present an inexplicable contrast in options for the public. Travellers were being encouraged to take a holiday, move house, join the army, or buy 'war loan.' The GCR was keen to induce people to take holidays in resorts served by its trains, including Blackpool, Buxton, Chester, Ramsey, Scarborough and Stratford, which it described as being 'suitable for all classes & requirements.' People wishing to buy a new house were exhorted to buy a copy of 'The Homestead' ('full of useful and valuable information'), but the greatest weight of advertising was aimed at raising money to finance the war. Purchasers of War Loan were offered 4½% interest, and were further prompted into investing by stirring appeals to the patriotic spirit. 'Back them up,' proclaim the posters,' and you will help your country and our brave troops in the fighting line.'

Facing page: Celebrity names synonymous with speed were invited to platform 10 at King's Cross to wish the crew well, when the first non-stop 'Flying Scotsman' of the season left London. On July 17 1933 Captain Geoffrey de Havilland, winner of the King's Cup Air Race, is pictured on the front of No. 4472 *Flying Scotsman* with Driver Bill Sparshatt and Fireman Smith, as departure time approached. There is no mistaking the prestige nature of this train: the headboard and the headlamps have a brilliant white finish and the only dirty marks on the platework are the dusty footprints made by the three men posing for the picture!

Above: Driver Jack Allen, of Doncaster shed, gives the press photographer a cheery wave from the cab of No. 2747 *Coronach* while he waits with Fireman Hazeldene to leave King's Cross with the accelerated 'Scarborough Flier' of July 8 1935. The 'Flier's' faster timing was the principal feature of the LNER's summer timetable for 1935: the train was retimed to cover the 188.2 miles between King's Cross and York in both directions in three hours, entailing a start-to-stop speed of 62.7mph. The York-Scarborough time remained unchanged at 50 min. In 1934 the LNER had already cut the London-York running time 3½ to 3¼ hrs. *Coronach*, built at Doncaster in 1928 and named after the 1926 winner of both the Derby and St Leger, had been the subject of an experiment when the top of the smokebox had been cut away and formed into a duct, with the aim of helping smoke lifting. The modification was not entirely successful — it was certainly unsightly — and the smokebox was restored to normal.

Right: On December 6 1935 King's Cross Stationmaster H. Ireland shakes hands with Driver G. Burfoot, on No. 2510 *Quicksilver*, as he prepares to leave with the evening's down 'Silver Jubilee' working. This train was normally worked by a King's Cross engine, which returned to London with the 'up' service of the following day. This was 50th such double-trip working and the LNER thus seized the opportunity to bill it as the '100th' run of the 'Silver Jubilee' and invited the press along to King's Cross for this picture. Three of the silver 'A4's' were based at 'Top Shed' for this prestige duty, the other being shedded at Gateshead, from where it worked as pilot at Newcastle as a reserve engine in case the King's Cross engine failed. Stationmaster Ireland had been promoted to King's Cross in 1932 from a similar job at Peterborough.

Left: The departure of the first non-stop 'Flying Scotsman' was an event which attracted maximum publicity and the train's two crews were undoubtedly the heroes of the day. On May 1 1928 a large crowd of well wishers gathered around No. 4472 *Flying Scotsman* as the departure time of 10am approached. In the cab, King's Cross Driver Albert Pibworth and Fireman Goddard await the green flag while relief crew Driver Blades and Fireman Morris, of Gateshead shed, are on the platform.

Below: The first non-stop 'Flying Scotsman' was met on arrival at King's Cross on May 1 1928 by LNER Chairman William Whitelaw, seen here in the inevitable bowler hat, presenting souvenirs of the occasion to Driver J.Day and Fireman Gray, who rolled the train into the terminus one minute early, at 6.14pm. The crew in charge for the first part of the journey from Edinburgh, Driver Henderson and Fireman McKenzie are standing in front of the smokebox door of 'Pacific' No. 2580 *Shotover*. The 'Flying Scotsman' headboard had been an idea of Haymarket shed men: North British local trains had for many years utilised destination headboards and one was hurriedly prepared for the 'Flying Scotsman.' Shortly afterwards King's Cross produced a similar one for their engines. This introduced headboards to British main line prestige trains for the first time.

Left: On the cushions. The third class compartment nearest to the engine on the non-stop 'Flying Scotsman' trains was reserved for the relief crew, the change-over usually taking place at the half-way point, just north of York. Here we see Driver Henderson and Fireman McKenzie catching up with the news after completing their stint on the footplate on August 20 1928. The eight-wheeled corridor tenders when loaded with nine tons of coal and 5,000 gallons of water weighed almost as much as two corridor coaches.

Right, above: It was suggested by railway enthusiast K.Risdon Prentice that the 100th 'Pacific' to be completed at Doncaster should be named after Sir Nigel Gresley, the LNER's eminent CME. This was agreed and when No. 4498 was ready to enter service it was formally named at a special ceremony at Marylebone on November 26 1937, at which Company Chairman William Whitelaw is seen presenting Gresley with a miniature silver replica of the engine. The LNER marketed small paperweight models of both the A3 and A4 classes, which were very popular. No. 4498 itself can still be seen and heard at work on the main line, being owned by the A4 Locomotive Society and is based at Steamtown, Carnforth together with 'A3' No. 4472 Flying Scotsman.

Right, below: Several of Sir Nigel's staff were present at the naming ceremony. From left to right they included. W.Massey; H.Harper (Chief Clerk); B. Spencer (Technical Assistant; : G.A. Musgrave (Locomotive Running Superintendent, Scotland); W.H. Brown (Carriage & Wagon Works Manager, York); D.R. Edge (C&W Works Manager, Doncaster); A.H.Peppercorn (Locomotive Running Superintendent, Southern Area); F.Wintour (retired 1927, was Doncaster Works Manager when Gresley was appointed Locomotive Superintendent of the GNR); Sir Nigel Gresley (holding model); R.A.Thom (Mechanical Engineer, Southern Area); O.V.S.Bulleid (Assistant to CME, later to become CME of the SR); H.Broughton (Chief Draughtsman); F.H.Eggleshaw (Locomotive Works Manager, Doncaster); E.Thompson (Mechanical Engineer, North Eastern Area); J.A.Street (Chief Locomotive Draughtsman).

Right: After Sir Ronald Matthews' appointment as LNER Chairman in 1938, a number of 'A4s' previously carrying the names of wild birds were renamed after Chairmen and Deputy Chairmen of the LNER, the Chairman of the Locomotive Committee (Andrew K.McCosh) and the Chief General Managers. When Sir Ralph Wedgwood retired as CGM in March 1939 his name was given to No. 4469 (previously *Gadwall*) at a ceremony at Marylebone. Wedgwood is pictured (left) with Sir Ronald Matthews, after the ceremony. No. 4469 was destroyed in an air raid at York in 1942 but Sir Ralph's name was then transferred to No. 4466 *Herring Gull*.

Left, above: C.H.Newton was appointed to succeed Sir Ralph Wedgwood on his retirement as CGM in March 1939. Newton had started his railway career on the GWR, later transferring to the GER. At the Grouping he became Assistant Chief Accountant of the LNER and this photograph shows him at his desk at King's Cross on taking up his appointment as Chief Accountant on June 5 1928. He transferred to general management in January 1936 when he became Divisional General Manager, Southern Area. He was knighted in 1943 and retired in June 1947 when he was appointed to the Board of the LNER. Miles Beevor succeeded him as CGM. 'A4' No. 4901, originally named *Capercaillie* was renamed *C.H.Newton* and finally *Sir Charles Newton*. It served in the BR fleet as No. 60005.

Left, below: A view of a busy booking office rarely seen by the passenger. In the days before ticket machines, the huge variety of pasteboard tickets for a wide range of destinations had to be carefully stacked in dozens of racks: to the right of the ticket clerk is the date-stamping machine and (hung on the edge of the rack) his ticket snips. Pieces would be snipped from the ticket to denote a child ticket, or forces or privilege tickets. A triangular piece cut from the top half of the ticket, for example, indicated that it had been issued to a woman. The scattered piles of old £5 notes on the clerk's right, and the £1 notes on his left would seem rather insecure today: The inscribed glass above the hatch indicates that this was a third class ticket window.

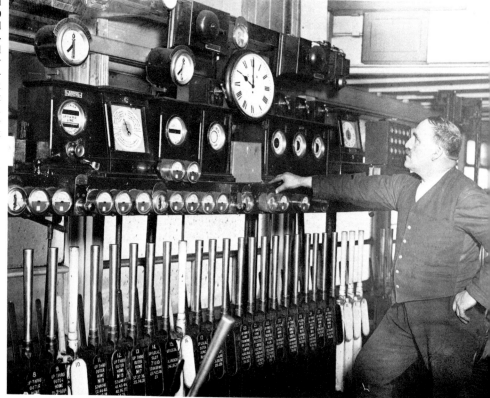

Right: Signalman Rogers waits in the Liverpool Street Station signal box for the centralised 10 o'clock time signal, sent out twice a day to all stations and signal boxes on the LNER network. LNER time was regulated to the second by these time checks, which was received by the single-needle morse code instruments provided in most station booking offices. Normal practice was that no messages would be sent after five minutes to ten until the signal had been received. The message consisted of the word 'ten' being spelt out, the time check being on the 'n.'

Above: A historic exchange of locomotives took place in May 1925 when an LNER 'Pacific' visited the Great Western Railway and a Swindon-built 'Castle' hauled trains between King's Cross and Doncaster. The LNER ambassador, seen here amidst large crowds at Paddington, was No. 4474 (later named Victor Wild), which ran three return trips to Plymouth with the 'Cornish Riviera Express,' alternating with a 'Castle' 4-6-0. The GWR engines produced better results, primarily because of shortcomings in the 'Pacific's' valve design which resulted in a throttling of the steam supply to the cylinders leading to unnecessarily high coal consumption. The valve travel on the 'Pacifics' was improved as a consequence, and higher pressure boilers were fitted. When, years later comparative testing took place under BR auspices between the 'A4s' and the GWR 'Kings,' the Gresley engines were shown to be superior performers.

THESE two views contrast the older type of manually operated signal box with the later electro-pneumatically operated system pursued by the LNER in the 1930s. The old King's Cross West box pictured above in May 1925 was built in 1881 with 140 levers, controlling the down side of the station, the suburban platforms and movements in the station yard. The signalmen worked in the traditional fashion, facing out across the tracks they controlled. A smaller manual King's Cross East Box controlled the up side of the terminus. The installation of the new signalling and control system at King's Cross was completed in 1933 and one larger box of 232 miniature levers (left) replaced both manual boxes. The new box was manned by four staff who faced a comprehensive track diagram, instead of looking out over the track. In a 24-hour period the box would control the movement of 800 trains and light engines at King's Cross, using more than 18,000 lever movements. The box operated 142 signal lights, nine route indicators and 69 point motors. It is pictured here on May 8 1953.

Above: The LNER had an imaginative and eye-catching policy towards poster advertising, and there were some superb examples. Some of these, especially those produced for the 'Silver Jubilee' have been reproduced as prints in recent years and make attractive decorations for the home. In March 1937 the LNER commemorated the centenary of the death of English artist John Constable by producing this special poster depicting the artist at one of his favourite locations; Flatford Mill. Note the use of Gill Sans lettering on the main notice board, although the older GNR pattern cast-iron notice on the left has yet to be replaced. March 31 1937.

Left: These press-button timetables were provided at King's Cross as early as May 1936 and the little notices below the information window tell the passenger 'Information free press button firmly.' The main line indicator board alongside was of the roller type, it being the duty of one of the platform staff to keep the information up to date at frequent intervals. it was easy to alter the information shown by pasting amendments over the original train details — there had evidently been a change to the stations served by the 12.40 (SO) to Cambridge, for example. The 12.00 departure was 'The Norse-man, Saturdays only commences 6th June, (Restaurant car) Newcastle Tyne Commission Quay. (Conveys boat passengers only). 'The neighbouring hoarding promoting 'Betta Biscuits' attracts customers with prices of 7d, 8d or 9d per lb for the various varieties!

Facing page: An impressive overall view of the interior of Liverpool Street station signal box, whose three signalmen controlled 165 signals. With the exception of New York Central station, Liverpool Street dealt with a greater peak load at this time than any other station in the world.

Above: A 'Pacific' locomotive working the non-stop 'Flying Scotsman' would use above 13,000 gallons of water on the 392½-mile of track between King's Cross and Edinburgh Waverley. The capacity of the tender was 5,000 gallons and this was replenished at water troughs en route, where the water was scooped up as the train ran along at speed. Six sets of troughs were installed between London and Edinburgh, and in this 1924 scene, workmen are cleaning out silt which has accumulated in the trough: another largely unseen job needed to ensure that the prestige trains continued running without a hitch.

Track maintenance today is a highly mechanised affair, complex and strangely shaped track machines bristling with hydraulic hoses and rams can tamp, level and slew the permanent way into the required profile very quickly indeed. In earlier years the quality of the permanent way depended on the skills and experience of gangers and platelayers working with manual tools. This series of photographs, taken from the 'Picture Post' magazine archives, owned by the BBC Hulton Picture Library, illustrate some of the work involved for the permanent way men.

Right: Darlington ganger Johnnie McGuirl tackles the monotonous but essential job of fishplate greasing in June 1950, removing the four bolts to enable the rail joint to be lubricated. The number of men needed for this type of work is easily imagined when you consider that where 60ft rails were in use a total of 88 joints per mile had to be periodically dismantled and greased — a total of 704 bolts per mile to deal with!

Right: Also in June 1950, Johnnie McGuirl (nearest camera) and his gang get to grips with a slewing job near the level crossing where the original S&DR crossed the NE main line, just north of Darlington Bank Top station. A married man with three children, Johnnie McGuirl was earning £4.15.6. for a 44-hour working week on the track, according to the original caption.

Left, above: In December 1955 a team led by Ganger Jim Dobson is busily at work changing sleepers on their Weeton length, between Harrogate and Leeds. The pick is being used to loosen the ballast prior to shovelling out, while the two men on the left are screwing a rail chair to a new sleeper. An auger was used for pre-drilling the sleepers, leaving piles of sawdust on the railchairs.

Left, below: Two of Jim Dobson's men put their muscles to work with crow-bars whilst a third member of the gang 'sights' along the rail to ensure that the curve and cant are constant and true. Today this work would be done by one man operating a specialised tamping, packing and slewing machine.

IN THIS book we have highlighted many facets of LNER equipment and operations, but it was the streamlined 'Pacifics' and their East Coast Main Line expresses which are best remembered, and as this album draws to a close we present a final reminder of these trains, engines and men.

Following the success of the 'Silver Jubilee', two years later the LNER introduced two more streamlined trains; the 'Coronation' between King's Cross and Edinburgh and the 'West Riding Limited' serving Leeds and Bradford. The new series of 'A4s' which followed the four 'silver' engines were at first painted green and given the names of wild birds, including *Golden Eagle* and *Kestrel*. However, it was decided that the 'Coronation' should be painted in distinctive two-tone blue livery and the locomotives liveried to match. Moreover, five of the new engines were named after important countries in the Commonwealth and British Empire, these being Nos 4485-92 *Union of South Africa*, *Dominion of Canada*, *Empire of India*, *Commonwealth of Australia* and *Dominion of New Zealand*.

No. 4492 *Dominion of New Zealand* was stationed at King's Cross almost all its life and is seen (facing page) drawing away from platform 5 in 1938. The observation car, pictured (above) leaving King's Cross on October 17 1938, was attached during the summer months and was turned at the end of each journey so that it was always at the end of the train. The 'Coronation' made the journey between the two capitals in six hours, with one stop in each direction. The down train reached York at an average speed of 71.9mph, the fastest start-to-stop schedule in Britain, a record held by the LNER until the streamlined services ceased in September 3 1939 when the Second World War broke out. In the late 1930s

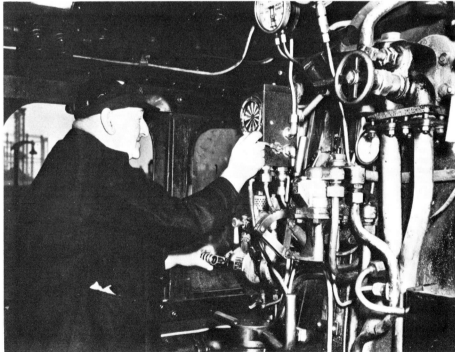

air travel had by no means achieved the reliability and popular appeal it enjoys today and a journey on one of the LNER 'streamliners' was the epitome of fast, comfortable travel. Indeed, to be able to boast in the 1930s that you had travelled on the 'Coronation' was the equivalent, in today's terms, of a flight on *Concorde*.

Above: This was the peak of many a schoolboy's dream: to sit in the driving seat of one of Gresley's express passenger locomotives. This picture, taken on October 27 1952, to illustrate new Automatic Train Control equipment, shows driver Jim Marshall of Grantham watching the road ahead. His left hand is holding the train vacuum brake application valve whilst his right rests on the ATC cancelling lever. The cranked handle at the bottom of the picture is the reversing screw and the brass wheel towards the top right is the steam valve for one of the injectors.

This photograph is a worthy tribute to the news photographers in general whose work has filled these pages: in particular it is a tribute to the creativity of the 'Picture Post' approach to photo-journalism. In gathering dusk on a winter's evening in 1955, Ganger Jim Dobson and his men load their tools onto a hand trolley beneath a tattered warning flag, after a hard day's 'graft' on their length at Weeton, near Harrogate. Whilst the prestige trains and the top link enginemen captured the public imagination, many thousands of railwaymen like these played a largely unseen but essential role. Without men like Jim Dobson, Johnnie McGuirl and their gangs (See pages 116-117), footplate heroes like Bill Sparshatt, Ted Hailstone and Bill Hoole would never have had their chance.